AF478143

BRITISH WEATHERVANES

GENERAL EDITOR
CHRISTINE BURGIN

BRITISH WEATHERVANES

R. GRAHAM

WITH
2 PLATES IN COLOUR
AND
16 ILLUSTRATIONS IN
BLACK & WHITE

WHITECHAPEL GALLERY   LONDON
CHRISTINE BURGIN   NEW YORK · DONALD YOUNG   CHICAGO
MMIX

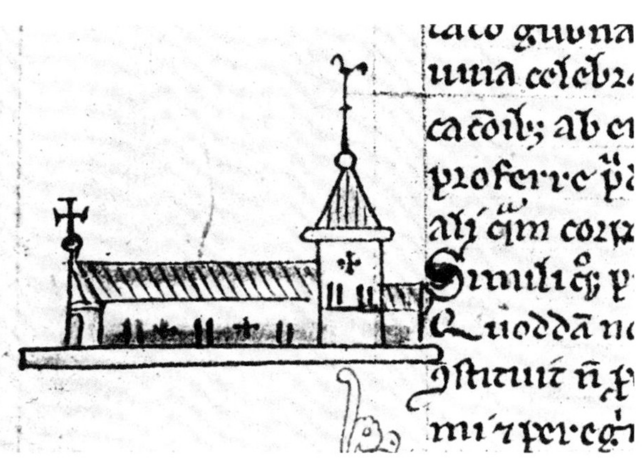

Weathercock of St. John's Hospital, Oxford.
Marginal drawing from a fifteenth-century manuscript

CONTENTS

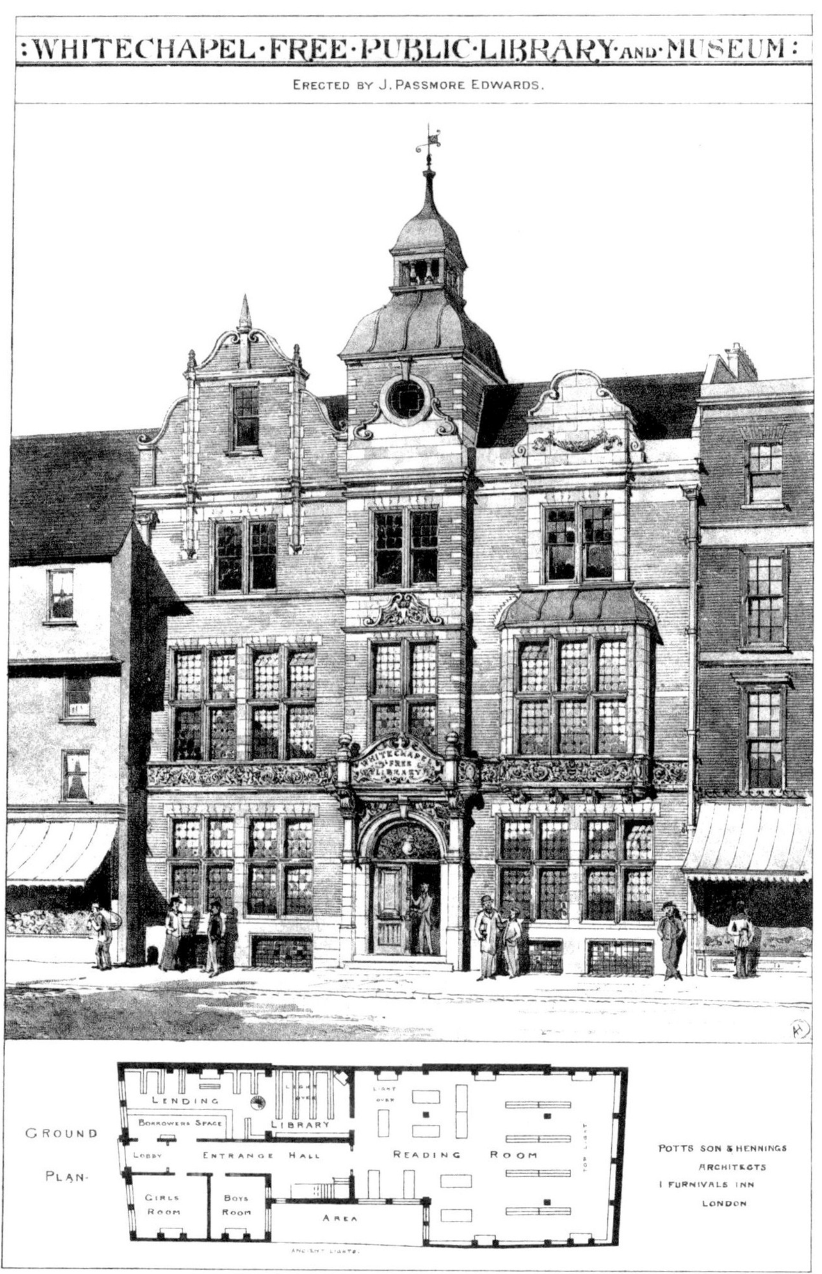

WHITECHAPEL FREE PUBLIC LIBRARY AND MUSEUM, 1892

'THE TRIP IS THE THING': RODNEY GRAHAM
Iwona Blazwick

Why are so many of Rodney Graham's trips circular? From film loops to weathervanes, his works embark on journeys that always go round in circles. This book is published to celebrate a work that not only revolves but also looks backwards while facing forwards. *Weathervane* (2007) features the silhouette of a handsome horse, head held high, in the spirit of the equestrian statue. Cast in copper the animal looks out across a prospect of rooftops and distant horizons. There are two installed versions of this work: one looks at the view across the city of Vancouver; the other, situated on the far side of the globe, gazes across the skyline of London gracing a newly expanded Whitechapel Gallery.

The horse and rider is a theme that has persisted in art, from antiquity until the modern era. There are twenty-five equestrian statues in London alone. Yet from the statuary of ancient Greece to London's public monuments to the history paintings of Napoleonic France, this genre signifies leadership and militarism. The powerful animal is a representation of the mastery of space and the force of nature. It is also a ceremonial device. The horse holds aloft, and is dominated by, man—in Europe, the leader of armies; in North America, the cowboy.

Yet in this contemporary manifestation, the rider does not look purposefully towards a horizon he will soon conquer. Rather he has mounted the horse backwards and is bent as if in prayer, over a book, oblivious to the view and to this genre's rhetoric of power.

The rider is Erasmus of Rotterdam. He is reading his seminal book 'The Praise of Folly'. Written in England at the home of Thomas More in 1509, it became an unexpected best seller when it was first printed in 1511. Taking religious pieties and superstition as its target, it represents one of the foundations of humanism and of the Enlightenment. The model for this figure is the artist himself, the latest in a series of personae he has adopted throughout his career. Costumed in sixteenth-century clothes inspired by Holbein's portrait of Erasmus, Graham mounted a dummy horse and photographed himself, to create another work of art, a life-sized light box. In its subject matter, this image and the Weathervane sculpture also reiterate Graham's concern with illumination and interpretation, emblematised here by the writings of Erasmus.

The horse must make its own way; its rider is busy thinking. Both are also at the mercy of the elements. Although Erasmus is a key figure in European society's move towards rationalism, the direction in which he rides is dictated solely by the unpredictability of the weather. Horse and rider go where the wind blows and then only in circles. They are revolving and directionless, their marvellous absurdity representing a kind of autonomy.

Graham has made two Weathervanes. One, an edition for Parkett magazine conceived in 2002, features the artist in silhouette riding a cycle backwards. This form of architectural decoration also shares with previous work his interest in semi-obsolete mechanical forms, like the camera obscura or the horse-drawn carriage. Built around the River Thames, London established its wealth through its dockyards. The direction of the wind was crucial for shipping, and weathervanes have ornamented the city's skyline since the sixteenth century. Superseded by the satellite, they are a vestige of a time when society and the elements were intimately engaged. The increasingly artificial environments that we construct for ourselves — air-conditioned malls and atriums — have led to a dangerous imbalance in this fundamental relationship. We deny nature at our peril.

The Erasmus Weathervane can be seen as a symbol of reconnection with the environment. It celebrates the secular but also the nonsensical. It is also an exhilarating embodiment of pure pleasure. One of the greatest musical films set in London is *Mary Poppins* (1964). The frustrated children of an Edwardian family, neglected by their wealthy but preoccupied parents, amuse themselves by torturing their nannies. When the weathervane of their neighbour, a retired sea captain, registers a dramatic change in the direction of the wind, their world is transformed. Literally descending from the sky, Mary Poppins, nanny *extraordinaire,* is blown into their lives. They exchange submission to authority and the worship of capital for flying kites and feeding pigeons.

The Whitechapel Gallery has undergone a dramatic expansion through the incorporation of a grand but abandoned library building. Rodney Graham unites these two historic buildings with this sculpture. It sits within the vernacular of public monuments yet is light, mobile, and symbolic of all the great virtues.

We are most thankful to the artist for his generosity and also to Christine Burgin, who has conceived, supported, and produced this wonderful publication; and to Donald Young, who played a key role in the delivery of the work and the making of this book.

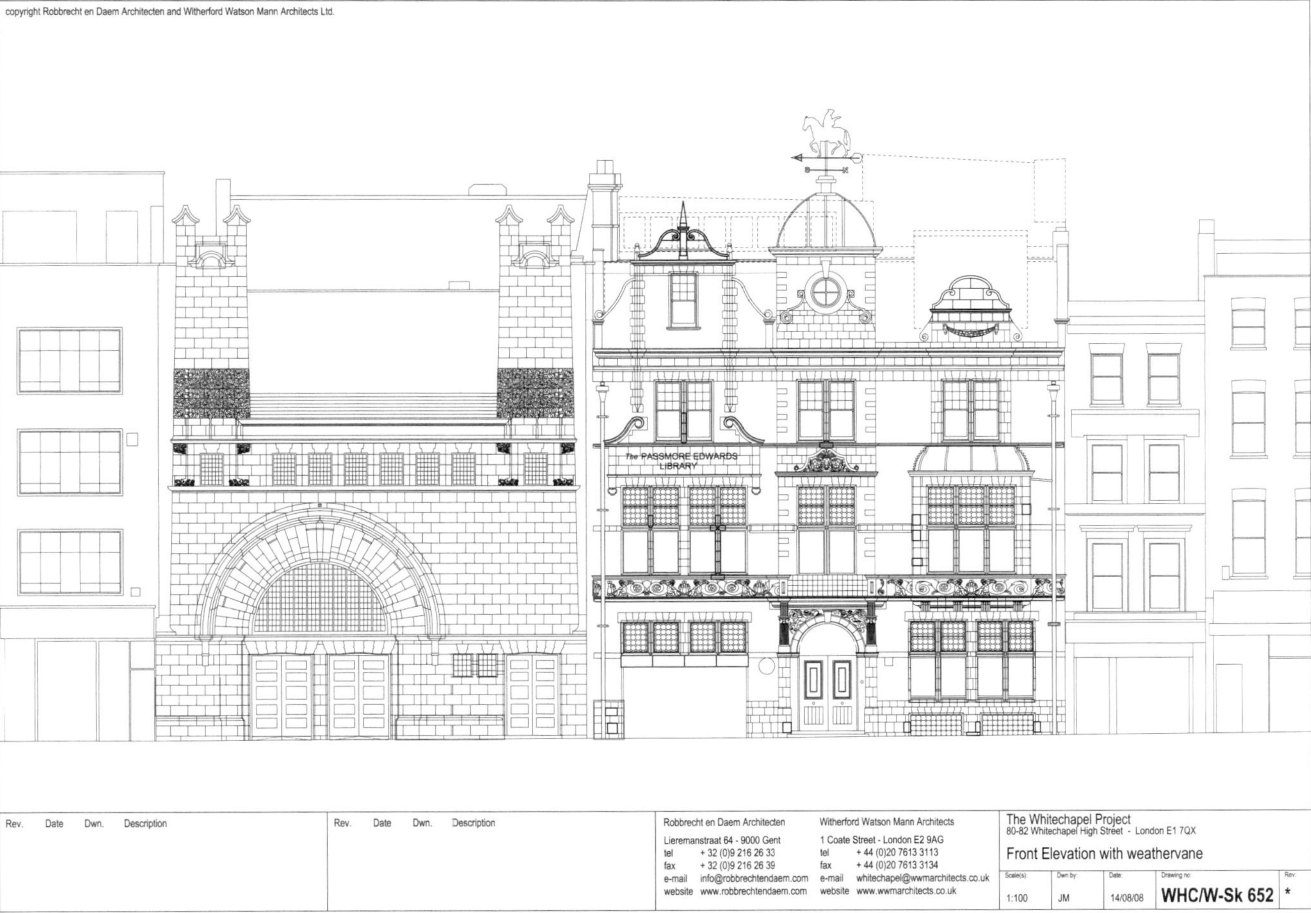

THE WHITECHAPEL PROJECT, 2009

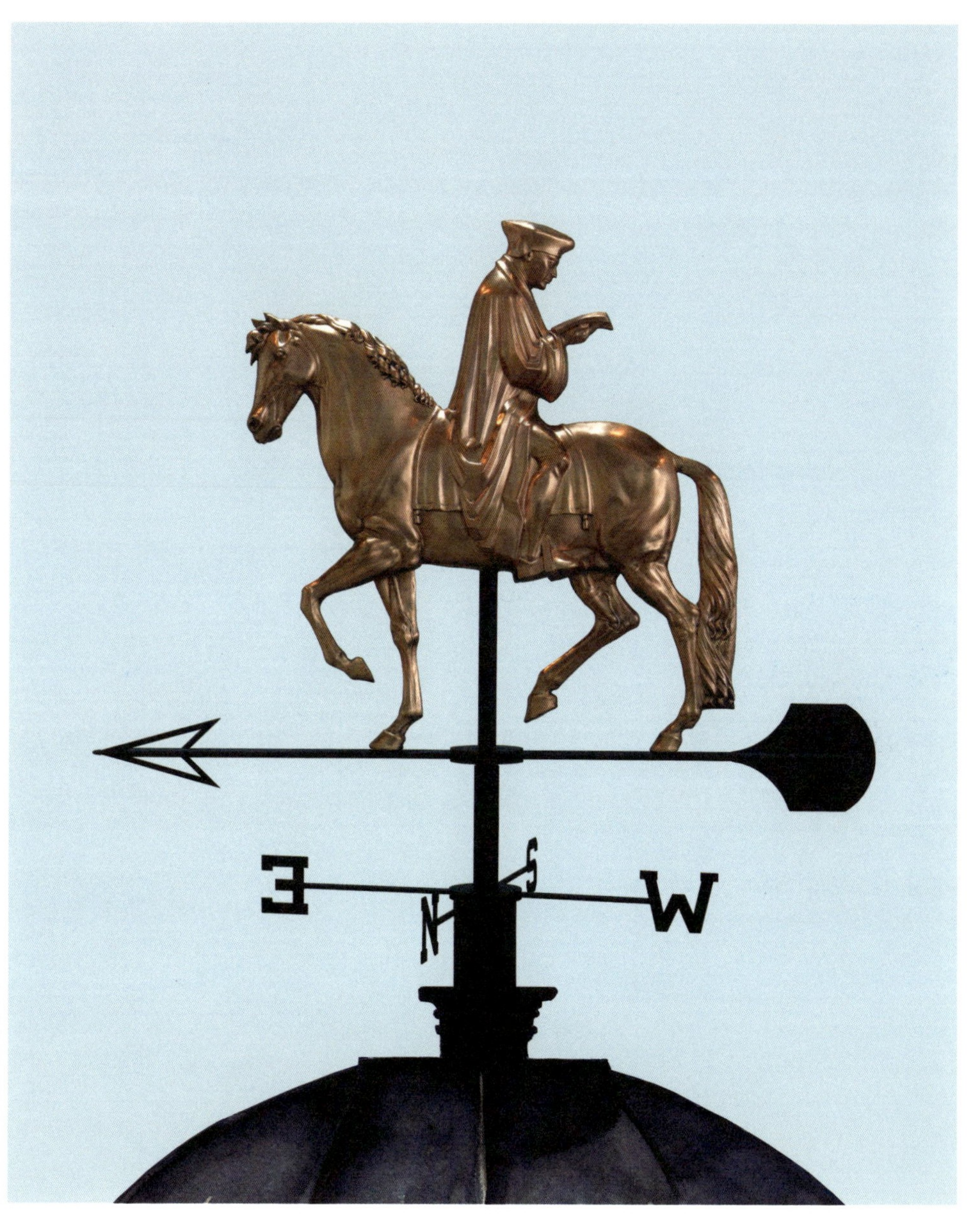

Weathervane (EAST), 2007
RODNEY GRAHAM

PONDERING ON HORSEBACK: THE PRAISE OF FOLLY
Candy Stobbs

Riding high above the rooftops of Whitechapel in East London is an unusual sight that awaits the casual viewer looking upwards for a moment from street to sky; a fifty-eight-inch-high bright copper sculpture appears of a historical-looking figure riding a lively horse, with a ringleted mane, reading a book whilst sitting backwards. The figure's back is to the wind. Closer investigation reveals this to be Rodney Graham's *Weathervane* sculpture, which depicts the artist dressed as the sixteenth-century humanist and classical scholar Erasmus. Absorbed in the solitary activity of reading, the figure is lost in thought and contemplation, not having to worry about where he is going or what lies ahead. As Rodney Graham puts it, he is able to 'ponder on horseback',[1] moving forward but also looking backwards, to the past.

Described as a 'serious dilettante', Graham wears a number of different hats, artist/musician/actor/writer, but in each sphere of activity his 'rigour and culture contain an intellectual curiosity that forces him to apprehend the structural foundations of the psyche and demands a mastery of the means that allow brilliant and lyrical variations on the inexhaustible theme of the Renaissance man'[2]. In light of this wide range of intellectual activity, figures from popular culture, including James Bond, Dr Seuss, Kurt Cobain, and Hollywood films interest him as much as Sigmund Freud, Stephen Mallarmé, or Raymond Roussell and can launch him into highly developed research-based projects. These have taken the form of books, slide shows, architectural models, musical compositions, and mobile camera obscuras as well as the more familiar formats of photography, painting, film, video, and sculpture.

Rodney Graham's weathervane is based on the account of the journey on horseback that Erasmus made from Italy to England about 1510, during which he wrote his best-known work, *The Praise of Folly*. Graham plays on the absurdism inherent in reading a philosophical treatise on human folly whilst riding on a horse backwards and continues his ongoing philosophical enquiry into cyclical and backward movement; like all his work it contains a complex narrative and is brimful of references—literary, philosophical, self-referential, and art historical. In describing the genealogy of the work, Graham mentions an advertisement he had noticed for an American insurance company which used an image of an American pilgrim reading a pamphlet on horseback, promoting its latest policies. Interested in making a public sculpture, Graham first made a lightbox study, *The Allegory of Folly: Study for an Equestrian Monument in the Form of a Wind Vane* (2005), in which he modelled himself on the figure of Erasmus. His costume and demeanour were based on a portrait by Hans Holbein (who later painted a celebrated full-length portrait of Erasmus' great friend and correspondent Sir Thomas More, to whom Erasmus was writing on this same journey). Later he asked an artist friend to make some drawings and sketches of a possible weathervane design which were used by a fine-art foundry to cast the weathervane in copper and the directionals in steel. Although often playing the central starring role in his works, Graham ceded the direction and in this case the design and production to others.

Rodney Graham's witty take on the classical equestrian monument was to raise it from its fixed stone or marble plinth and weighty presence on solid ground and transform it into an airbourne monument of copper and steel, with all the weathervane's 'allegorical suggestions of moving with the wind'[3], and which like 'folly goes against the grain'[4]. Graham's equestrian sculpture sits lightly and equally nobly in the air. Performing both as a functional—if charmingly outmoded device in our digitally determined world—working weathervane and as a visual pun on 'going nowhere', it celebrates the pleasures of literary absorption and the acquisition of knowledge and understanding; like Pegasus, the winged horse, it is capable of transporting us on 'flights of fancy'. A characteristically playful and multi-layered work, it refers back to earlier works, in particular a domestic-scale weathervane that Graham made for Parkett Editions in 2002 of a figure (clearly the artist) riding a bicycle sitting casually on the handlebars and facing backwards. This in turn refers to *Phonokinetoscope* (2002), based on the famous story of Albert Hofmann, the inventor of LSD, who experimented with his new chemical invention for the first time in 1943 whilst riding home on a bicycle. Graham, however, in reenacting this journey around the Tiergarten in Berlin, also after ingesting LSD, rides his bicycle backwards, allowing perhaps for more ruminative meandering experiences. As Lynne Cooke puts it: 'These free-wheeling trips serve as veiled analogues for mental flights'[5].

Taking part in Rodney Graham's ongoing empirical investigation into perception, consciousness, and rationality is a long cast list of *dramatis personae* that he has assumed, ranging from generic stereotypes from twentieth-century popular cinema—cowboys, castaways, and convicts—to historical and modern figures, all represented by Graham, literally and figuratively, in large-format photographic work. He first adopted what he calls 'the actor's position'[6] in *Halcion Sleep* (1994), when he began to place himself, the artist, at the forefront of his work as the central performer by creating scenarios dependent on his passive and active participation in the work. In *Halcion Sleep,* he knocked himself out with the sedative of the same name and is filmed sleeping in the back of a moving car by night as a cinematic but vague landscape passes by to which he remains oblivious in his blissed-out state.

Acknowledging himself as a performance artist, Graham has adopted the roles of historical and more contemporary characters, and this has become 'an unconscious thread' in his work, beginning in earnest with his cinematic 'costume drama trilogy'. Expensively produced to emulate Hollywood's high production values, it included Graham himself in three different scenarios taken from cinematic genres, the first of which, *Vexation Island* (1997), can be described as a 'tragedy', the second, *How I Became a Ramblin' Man* (1999), a 'Western', and *City Self/Country Self* (2000), in which he plays two roles, that of the eighteenth-century city dandy and country bumpkin, 'a comedy'.

Each of the three films is presented using a continuous loop mechanism, which Graham first used as a purely functional and practical device to display film and video work in a museum or gallery environment, where the viewer can drop in and pick up at any moment. This has since led him to explore themes of circularity and repetition, what Freud refers to as 'the compulsion to repeat'. In *Vexation Island* the marooned buccaneer is doomed to relive ad infinitum the sequence of finding himself on a pristine white sandy beach with only a parrot for company and an encounter with a falling coconut which delivers him unconscious, only to wake up finding himself on a pristine white sandy beach, etc. The singing cowboy in *How I Became a Ramblin' Man* rides into and out of a classic Western landscape in which nothing happens but his eternal return. In *City Self/ Country Self,* the build up to the *coup de grâce* in which the country bumpkin is humiliated by the city sophisticate consists of a series of scenes in which the attention to period detail is meticulous and the action presaged by a pocket watch and bell tower clock showing the time before the film returns to the country self arriving in the city and the circular pattern of looped time begins again. In a similar way, the weathervane can be seen to follow its own self-enclosed loop as its rotational axis means it can't go anywhere but within its prescribed circuit. What Sara Krajewski refers to as an invitation to 'ruminate on the cyclical nature of being'[7] is inherent in the circularity of the arcs described by Erasmus and his horse. Graham used the loop not only as a device in his film and video works but also in earlier text pieces in which he extended, and in turn complicated, passages in Ian Fleming's *Casino Royale* and in the nineteenth-century novella *Lenz* by George Büchner as well as in a musical composition, Richard Wagner's *Parsifal.* Again, these looping devices only lead back to the start, creating a self-contained world defined by the absence of any kind of ending or, in narrative terms, resolution.

Forming part of the immediate visual appeal of the weathervane is Graham's 'devotion to absurd incident'[8] and often Laurel and Hardy–type buffoonery, present in the comic, almost slapstick misadventures befalling the hapless characters in *Vexation Island, City Self/Country Self,* and *A Reverie Interrupted by the Police* (2003) in which Graham, dressed as a convict in striped prison garb, attempts to play the piano whilst wearing handcuffs. This sense of the absurd, in which the high seriousness of literary and philosophical endeavour is combined with visual comedy, is heightened by our awareness of Erasmus, that most worthy sixteenth-century philosopher and anti-clerical figure portrayed in an unexpected manner, whilst reading *The Praise of Folly,* one of the most influential texts of the early sixteenth century. In an earlier photographic work, *Fishing on a Jetty* (2000), Graham restages a scene with Cary Grant from Alfred Hitchcock's classic *To Catch a Thief,* in which there are many complex layers of reference to deception, duplication, the Vancouver art scene, and still-life painting but with a lightness of touch so that the prevailing humour of his approach is maintained. As Lynne Cooke describes it, 'the insidious wit underpinning this fictional/factual, literal/ metaphorical elision imbues the hallucinatory image with the distilled, compact character of a visual pun'[9].

Rodney Graham's poetic and humourous weathervane, helpfully indicating the wind direction and compass points for any serious traveller who looks upwards to contemplate the conditions for travel, continues his preoccupation with un-urgent journeying. Erasmus travels leisurely from Italy to England by horseback, the cowboy meanders gently off the beaten track, the buccaneer's unknown voyage throws him up on a 'treasure island', and the chemically-induced journeys that take place in the artist's head remind us even if we are not going anywhere in particular, 'the trip is the thing'[10].

Notes

1. Rodney Graham, conversation with Iwona Blazwick, Whitechapel Gallery, London, October 14, 2008.

2. Joseé Belislé, 'Brilliantly Paradoxical Work', in *Rodney Graham,* Musee d'art contemporain de Montreal, 2007.

3. Graham, conversation with Blazwick.

4. Ibid.

5. Lynne Cooke, 'A Can of Worms', in *Rodney Graham: A Little Thought,* Art Gallery of Ontario, Toronto, 2004, p. 66.

6. Rodney Graham, conversation with Blazwick.

7. Sara Krajewski, 'The Trip Is the Thing: The Cinematic Experience in Rodney Graham's Films' in *Rodney Graham: A Little Thought,* p. 32.

8. *Rodney Graham: A Little Thought,* Art Gallery of Ontario, Toronto, 2004.

9. Cooke, 'Can', p. 63.

10. Rodney Graham in *Rodney Graham,* Whitechapel Art Gallery, London, 2002, p. 109.

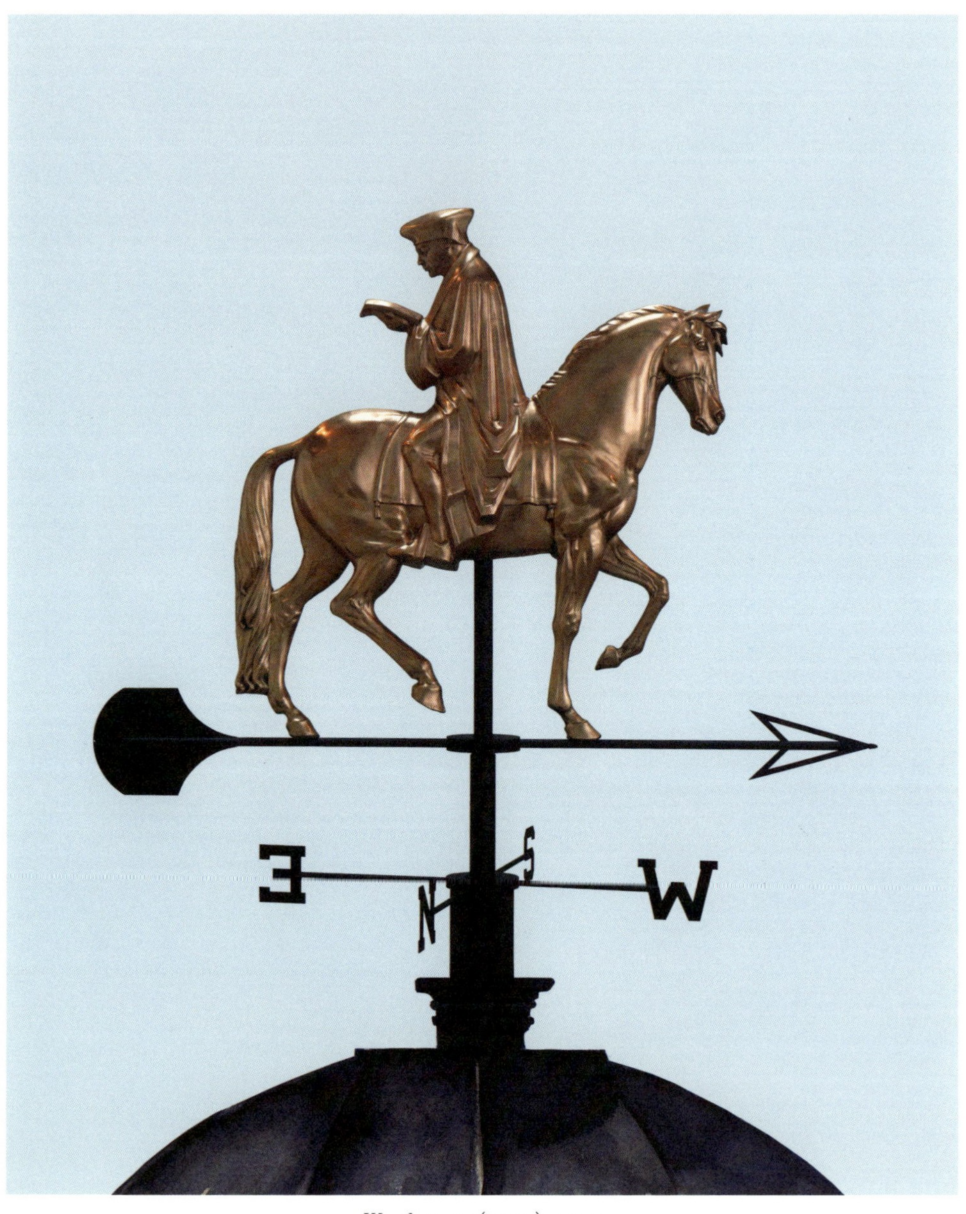

Weathervane (WEST), 2007
RODNEY GRAHAM

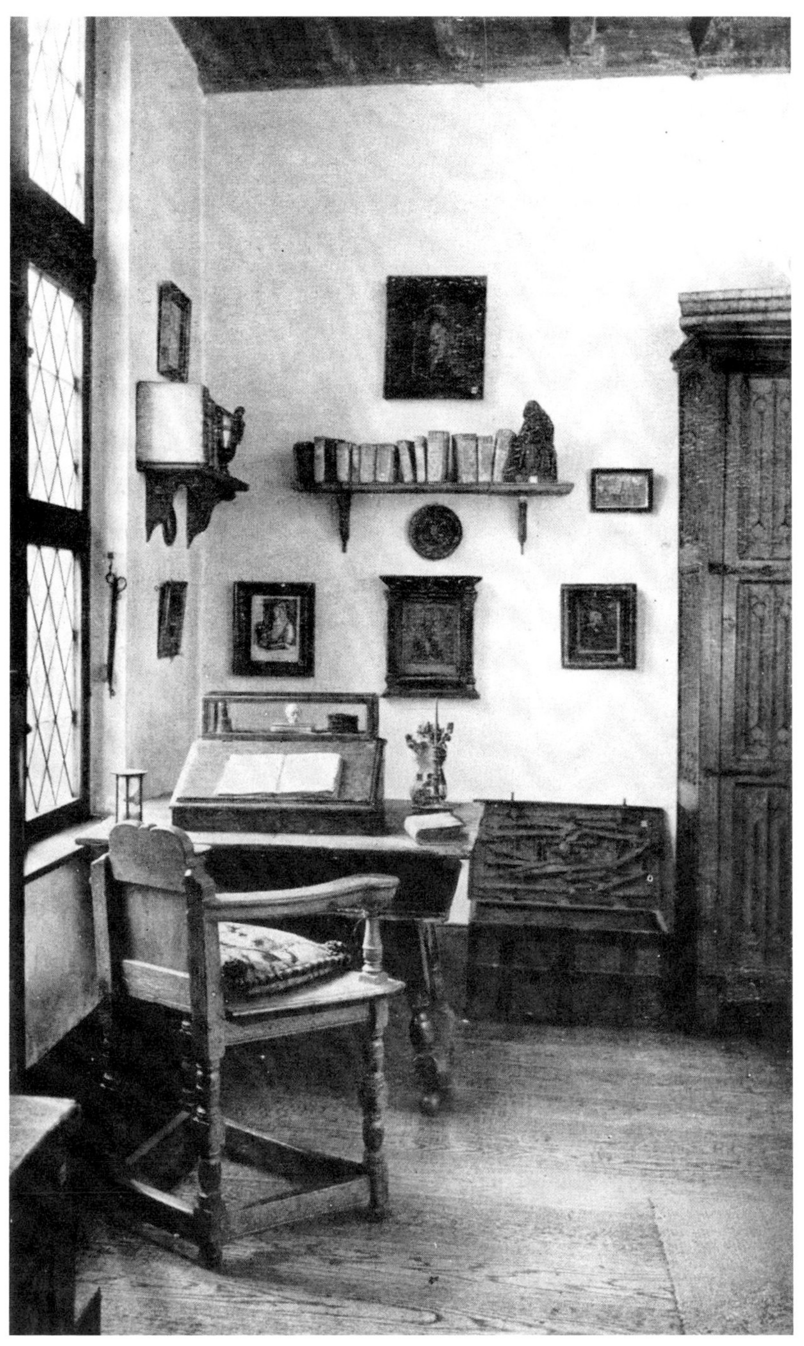

Erasmus' study at Anderlecht

THE TRAVELLING SCHOLAR
John Slyce

Certain essential aspects of the world are accessible only to laughter.
—MIKHAIL BAKHTIN, *RABELAIS AND HIS WORLD*

The reference library, where my thoughts were to rage,
I ate book after book, page after page.
I scoffed poetry for breakfast and novels for tea.
And plays for my supper. No more poverty.
Welcome young poet, in here you are free
To follow your star to where you should be.

That door of the library was the door into me

And Lorca and Shelley said, 'Come to the feast.'
Whitechapel Library, Aldgate East.

—BERNARD KOPS, FROM
WHITECHAPEL LIBRARY,
ALDGATE EAST

For Bakhtin, medieval Latin humour found its final and complete expression at the highest level of the Renaissance in Erasmus' *The Praise of Folly.* It is there one finds perhaps the greatest creation of carnival laughter in all world literature. In late medieval and especially Renaissance times, folly *was* taken as universal. This perspective, transmitted through the influence of Erasmus and his writings, was to have a profound effect on not only the comedy of Rabelais but also, one might argue, on the conciliatory comedy of Shakespeare.

Like the French noun *folie*, the term *folly* encompassed a great breadth of meaning and uses incorporating madness, mental derangement, and insanity alongside behaviour regarded as vain, improvident, and frivolous. In the consciousness of the period, folly imbricates the natural human condition and affects man as indiscriminately as death, all while connoting, in equal measure, sexual excitement and love, Christian or Socratic wise folly, and the artificial folly of the court fool.

It is a twenty-first-century weathervane now perched on what was once a cupola housing an empty plinth above the Whitechapel Library which provides me opportunity to explore correspondences between the figures of the travelling scholar, holy fools, and itinerant artists. Each shares something of a radical independence from the tenured embrace of an institution and yet each relies, in no small way, on tangential relations to, and direct and material contact with, the product of the concomitant worldly institutions in the library with its books, the marketplace as a stage, and those more or less disparate and at times public platforms on which one may present work and findings. This essay may, too, through its digressions, touch on elements of a short history of the humanist tradition and nineteenth-century philanthropy of a special type. The personages of D. Erasmus, J. Passmore Edwards, and one R. Graham each play their parts respectively as they meet in the reading room of the Whitechapel Library at a dramatic moment shaped by a stereoscopic vision of the past and present held in a single double focus, which constitutes, in itself, a humanist perspective and concern. Theirs is an imaginary conversation and suspended in the rivers of time—neither of today and our present moment, not lodged in the past, or even projected into a distant future. Others who inhabit their own here and now will inevitably make uses and meanings gleaned from the exchange, but these will belong to tomorrow and the book.

J. Passmore Edwards funded the creation of some twenty-four public libraries spread between London and Cornwall, though the majority of these served the people of London's East End. Downstairs is a scrolled tablet commemorating the tycoon philanthropist who saved and endowed the Whitechapel Library when its founders' funds ran out. At the opening ceremony, Edwards spoke: 'I think it is a distinguishing privilege to assist in lightening and brightening the lot of our East End fellow-citizens.... I have long felt that the East End of London has stupendous uncancelled claims on the wealthy and well-to-do people of West London.' At the time, Edwards could know nothing of 'The Whitechapel Boys' who would arrive at its reading room, nor how this building and its holdings would come to be referred to as 'the university of the ghetto'. He did know something of the thirst for and pursuit of knowledge under difficulties, and in his autobiography he writes how he would have 'jumped with joy if I could have found a corner in a reading-room for an hour or two a day, or have been enabled to take books home as boys and girls can now where public libraries exist.'

The Greeks' city-states embraced the ideal of *paideia* long before the term *humanism* came into being and was popularized in the nineteenth century to refer to cultural change that had occurred half a millennium before. This ideal combined literary culture, piety, and social discipline towards achieving effective civic participation. The Latin equivalent of *paideia,* or *humanitas,* supplemented and added elements more appropriate to a Roman context: ideas of self-correction and self-cultivation constituting a central irreducible core that rendered the cultured individual independent of circumstances and yet exemplary for other men. The idea and value of a life of the mind, not to mention the museum without walls, arises from forces of cultural change and adaptation the autodidact feels with great sensitivity and knows intimately.

Passmore Edwards believed in public libraries because:

They are educative, recreative and useful; because they bring the products of research and imagination, and the stored wisdom of ages and nations, within easy reach of the poorest citizens; because they distribute without curtailing the intellectual wealth of the world; because they encourage seekers after technical knowledge, and thereby promote industrial improvement; because, being under public eye, they are economically conducted; because they teach equality of citizenship, and are essentially democratic in spirit and action, in as much as they are maintained out of the public rates and subject to public control All may not use them, but all may do so if they like; and as they are means of instructing and improving some, all are directly or indirectly benefited by them.

I suspect Edwards also knew the metafigural magic of a library as a transformative space where, with book in hand, a figure of a figure may be erected through dialogues struck internal to the reader and then also with myriad characters inhabiting the present, past, and future drawn in words upon the page. (This process can, of course, happen while seated in a chair or likewise even on horseback). Isaac Rosenberg no doubt made use of such allegorical adventures while warming himself in the reading room in the years before his death at the Somme. And Weinstein, Lefkowitz, Bomberg, and Gertler, too, must have travelled this wordly portal with its projections and welcome supplements to what would otherwise be only bricks and mortar.

Passmore Edwards's philanthropy was indeed Late Roman from Ancient Greek in that his support aimed to foster a reader with a capacious mind, balanced judgment, and the capacity to fulfil with propriety all the offices of private and public life, yet his love of man and gift was far more than that. The public library—and no less, the public museum or art gallery—still represents an ideal of autodidactic self-improvement in that it offers a community based on knowledge and ideas rather than private inheritance or bloodlines. This is the case as long as each remains free, friendly and open to all.

It might be thought that I have said far too little of the man for all seasons and a weathervane for all climes. However, like many old and ancient ideas, humanism is a wildly elastic term and I fear I may have already stretched its garment further than is wise. Having gone thus far, I will ask you to indulge my excesses only a very little more. If I have underplayed an essential note here, it is that of human-to-human communication. A book, a picture, any work of art—even that crafted as a weathervane—comes to life in words, speech, conversation, and dialogue. Communication is to humanism in much the same animated and co-dependent relationship. Each is only ever a medium and relies on mediation provided by you and me to move, just as a weathervane will tell a very different story when deprived of the wind. If I seem to have created a puzzle, I do so only in a foolish attempt to stress what could be far more elegantly and economically said in quoting Georges Perec: 'The parts do not determine the pattern, but the pattern determines the parts.' Language is the best and only weapon of humanism. Erasmus' own rise was through that of the written word, and the self-same produced his fall. It was equally the printed word that brought a close to Erasmus' own long winter and that of humanism. Whether printed or illuminated, the freely circulating word is perhaps still the best weapon with which to oppose pomposity, self-aggrandisement, malice, and greed. And with that I should end, bearing only a faltering hope that I have managed to write even something to the point.

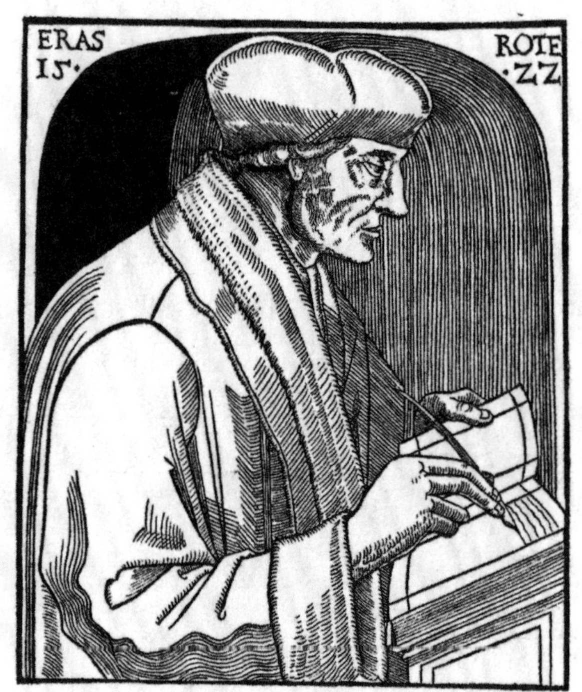

Anonymous, Portrait of Desiderius Erasmus, 1522

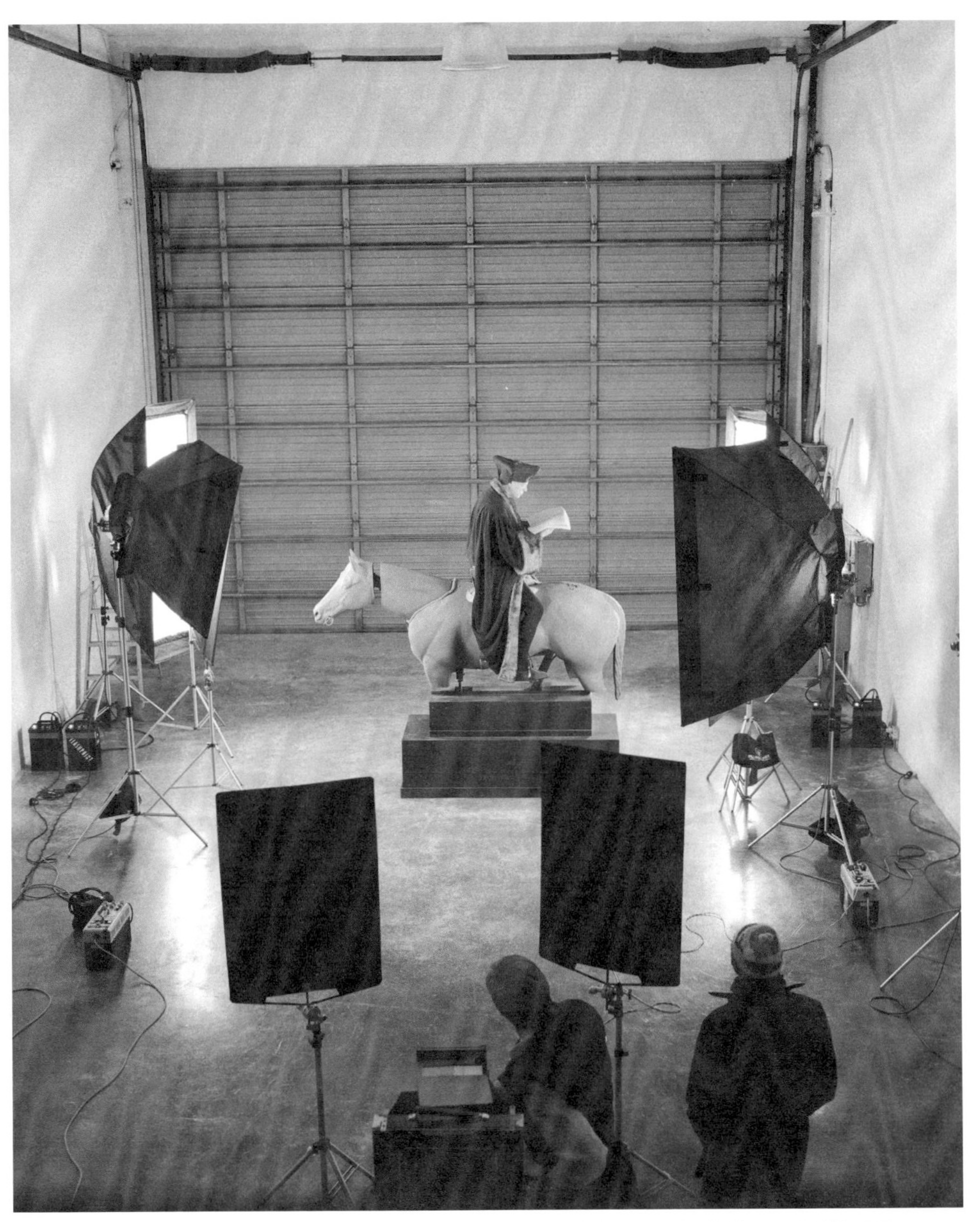

Preface to *The Allegory of Folly: Study for an Equestrian Monument in the Form of a Wind Vane*
Rodney Graham

Desiderius Erasmus of Rotterdam
to
his friend Thomas More [1]

PREFACE TO *THE PRAISE OF FOLLY*

Recently when I was on my way from Italy to England, instead of wasting all the time I had to spend on horseback in idle chatter and empty gossip, I tried occasionally to think over some of the things we have studied together, and to call to mind the conversation of my most learned and agreeable friends from whom I was then separated.

Among those friends, you, my dear More, were the first whose name occurred to me, since I find just as much pleasure in thinking of you when we are apart as I do in your company when we are together. And, upon my soul, nothing in life has ever brought me more pleasure than your friendship. Well, since I felt I must be doing something, and the circumstances were hardly proper for serious study, I thought I might occupy myself with the praise of folly. What put such a notion in my mind? you may ask. My first hint came from your family name More, which is just as close to Moria, the Greek word for folly, as you are remote from the thing itself. In fact, everyone agrees that you're as far removed from it as possible. Besides, I had a suspicion that this joke would be agreeable to you because you particularly enjoy jests of this sort—that is, if I don't flatter myself, jests seasoned with a touch of learning and a dash of wit. For that matter, you enjoy playing the role of Democritus in all the common business of life. [2] Though as a result of your searching and original mind you're bound to hold opinions very different from those of common men, yet by virtue of your warm and sincere manner you can get along with all sorts of people at any time of day, [3] and actually enjoy doing so. Will you then accept this little declamationlet of mine as the keepsake of a friend, and take it under your protection? For now that it is dedicated to you, it is properly yours, not mine. I don't doubt that there will be busybodies to condemn the book, some saying that it's composed of trifles too silly to befit a theologian's dignity, others declaring that it's too sharp of tooth [4] to accord with the modest behavior of a Christian—they will thunder out comparisons with the Old Comedy and the satires of Lucian, [5] they will say I snap and slash at everyone like a mad dog.

23

Well, will the people who are offended by the frivolity of the argument and the absurdity of the jokes kindly reflect that I'm not setting the style here? The same thing has been done before, again and again, by famous authors of the past.[6] It was centuries ago that Homer toyed with his "War Between the Frogs and the Mice," Virgil with his "Gnat" and his "Garlic Salad," Ovid with his "Nut." Polycrates wrote in praise of Busiris the tyrant, and Isocrates, though no friend to Polycrates, did the same thing; Glaucon spoke up for injustice. Favorinus praised Thersites and the quartan ague, Synesius had words to say in favor of baldness, and Lucian wrote panegyrics on a fly and a parasite. Seneca ridiculed Claudius in his *Pumpkinification,* Plutarch wrote a dialogue in which Ulysses disputed with a hog, Gryllus, both Lucian and Apuleius wrote about life as seen by an ass, and some anonymous author wrote the last will and testament of a hog named Grunnius Corocotta, of which Saint Jerome preserved a recollection.[7]

If it makes them any happier, let the complainers imagine that I spent my travel-time playing chess or riding on a hobby-horse. Every other profession is entitled to a bit of leisure—what's so terrible if scholars take a little time off for play, especially if their foolery leads to something slightly more serious? Some jokes can be managed in such a way that a Reader who isn't altogether thick of nose can profit by them—more, perhaps, than from the pompous formal arguments of certain people we know. I have in mind some paltry fellow who patches up an oration in praise of rhetoric or philosophy, or another supple rascal who's set on flattering his prince, or some agitator who wants to rouse up everyone to go off and fight the Turk. There are fools who pretend to predict the future and others who strain to settle some subtle and difficult point that doesn't matter a fraction of a trifle either way. Just as it's the height of triviality to treat serious matters in a trivial way, so there's nothing more delightful than finding that some trifles have been managed so that they turn out far from trivial. About my own performance it's not for me to judge; but unless I'm completely misled by 'self-love,' my praise of folly hasn't been performed altogether foolishly.

Now let me answer those cavilers who object to what they call biting satire. Good wits have always been allowed the liberty to exercise their high sprits on the common life of men, and without rebuke, as long as their sport doesn't become savagery. That's why I'm so impressed by the delicacy of modern ears which can scarcely endure anything but formal titles of honor. You can even find some religious men so topsy-turvy in their values that they listen more complacently to real blasphemies against Christ than to the mildest of jokes about the pope or the local prince, especially if the joke might 'touch them in the pocketbook'. But if someone attacks the vices of human kind without mentioning any individual by name, is he harming people or rather teaching them? Admonishing them? Consider in addition on how many scores I attack my own self. Beside, when men of every different sort are censured, it's clear that vice in general is the target, not a particular person. So if anyone complains that he's been harmed, it's either his conscience that accuses him or his guilt. Saint Jerome wrote in this vein much more freely and bitterly, sometimes not even suppressing personal names.[8] I have not only avoided naming people, but have softened my style so that any intelligent reader will understand my intention was to divert, not to insult. Unlike Juvenal, I made no effort to rake in the sewer of hidden crimes;[9] my aim was to ridicule absurdities, not to catalogue sins. And if there's someone who can't be calmed by these reflections, let him recall that it's a kind of compliment to be attacked by Folly; when I chose her as my spokesperson, I was bound to observe the proprieties of her character. But why do I say all these things to you, who are so skilled an advocate that even in causes that aren't the best, you can put up the best defence? Farewell, most learned More, and defend your Folly faithfully.

From the country, June 9, 1510 [10]

Notes

1. The son of a London judge and a practicing attorney himself, More in 1510 was about thirty-three years old, thus some ten years younger than Erasmus. In sharp contrast to his older friend, who remained celibate all his life, More had committed himself to a secular career and had married; he was already the father of three children. Intellectually and socially, More and Erasmus were immediately and deeply sympathetic. Both were scholars in the humanist tradition with a special interest in Greek, both were witty ironists, both recognized the need for liberal reforms in church and state. Their first meeting was in 1499, when Erasmus visited England at the invitation of a former pupil, Lord Mountjoy, whom he had known in Paris; it was therefore inevitable that when Erasmus came north again in 1509, he should stay with More.

2. Though primarily significant as a physicist and mathematician, Democritus (of the fifth century B.C.) was popularly known as the "laughing philosopher" in contrast to Heraclitus, the "weeping philosopher."

3. The Latin is *omnium horarum hominemagere,* and it is adapted from the "Life of Tiberius" (42) by Suetonius. Its meaning there is distinctly disreputable; it implies a man who can drink night and day. Erasmus applies it with a very different meaning to More, and a man named Whittinton translated it in 1520 as "a man for all seasons"—hence the title of a popular play by Robert Bolt (1966) where the implications are not only laudatory but saintly.

4. More is concerned that his jest not be thought excessively cynical in spirit; the cynical philosophers got their name from the Greek word for dog, *kune.* The talk about sharp teeth and snapping at people all plays on the basic metaphor of a vicious dog.

5. Old Comedy (as in Aristophanes) attacked people by name; New Comedy (as Menander) represented general types. Erasmus' *Praise of Folly* could not possibly be compared to Old Comedy; but it does come very close to the dialogues of Lucian, known as "the scoffer"

and sometimes as "the atheist." By joining an absurd charge with one that might have some substance, Erasmus is able to dismiss them both.

6. Among the predecessors, Erasmus mingles examples of the mock-epic with those of the mock-panegyric. The examples attributed to Homer, Virgil, and Ovid were in fact by later parodists of the great poets. Busiris was a semi-mythical tyrant (i.e., Pharaoh) of Egypt, Isocrates the greatest Greek orator of his day. Glaucon was the brother of Plato, who in *Republic* 2 makes him speak for injustice in order to set up Socrates' rebuttal.

7. Thersites was the ugliest and least heroic of all the Greeks at Troy; Aulus Gellius (*Noctes Atticae* 17.12.2) tells how Favorinus wrote mock-orations praising both Thersites and the quartan fever, which we now call malaria. Seneca's piece mocking the deification of Claudius is really quite funny. The fantasies of Plutarch, Lucian, and Apuleius, all involving metamorphosis, have only this in common with the other works cited, that they are written in a "low" comic style. The will of Grunnius Corocotta the swine is a real oddity of the subliterature, a third-century joke for school children.

8. Saint Jerome, most erudite and least saintly of the early church fathers, was noted, if not always admired, for his strident polemical tone.

9. Juvenal (of the first century A.D.), bore the reputation of a harsh and biting satirist of ancient Rome, by contrast with his predecessor Horace, who wrote more light and amusing verses.

10. Early editions give the date as 1508, which is impossible, since Erasmus could not have described his sojourn in More's house before he arrived there in the second half of 1509. The date may be an accident, a joke, or a deliberate misstatement; but if the preface was written under the circumstances it describes, 1510 is the first possible date. Nobody knows where "in the country" was.

25

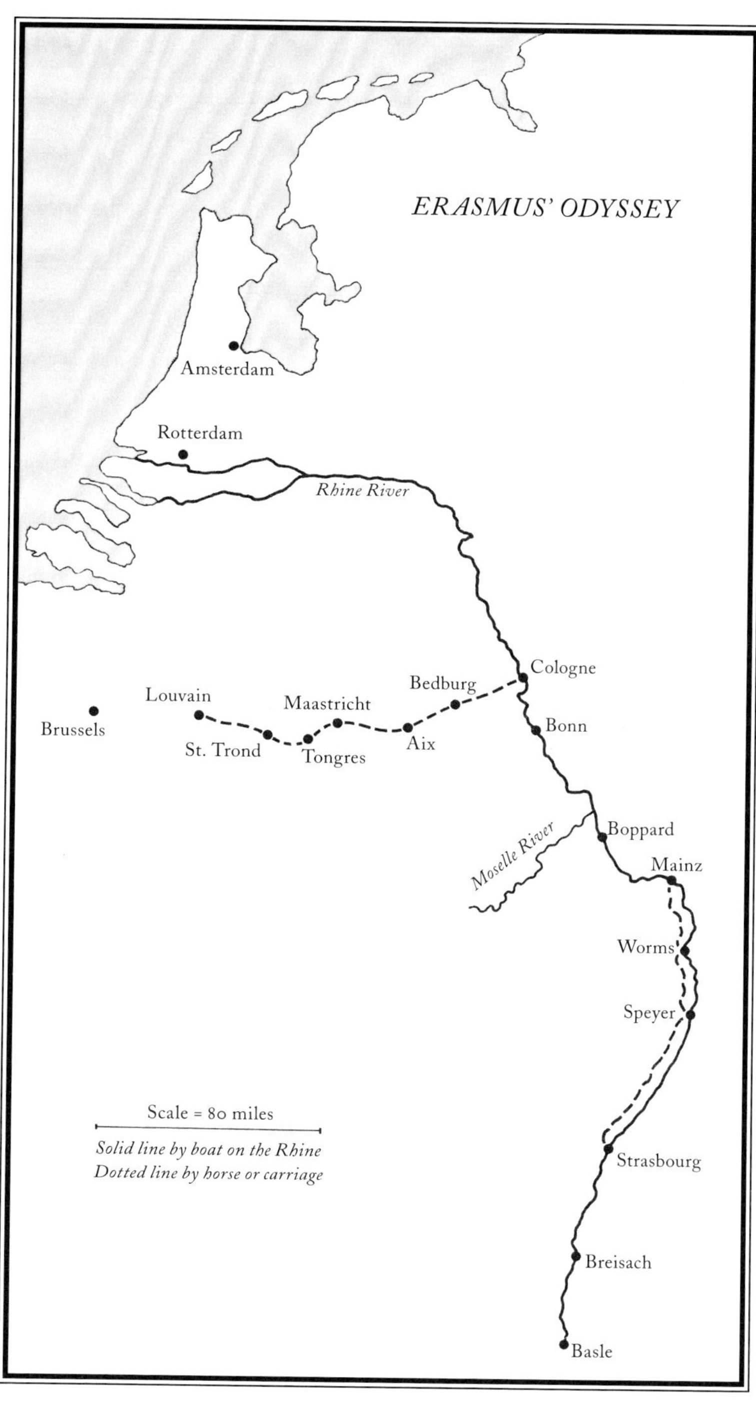

ERASMUS' ODYSSEY
Amsterdam
Rotterdam
Rhine River
Louvain
Brussels
Maastricht
Bedburg
Cologne
St. Trond
Tongres
Aix
Bonn
Moselle River
Boppard
Mainz
Worms
Speyer
Strasbourg
Breisach
Basle
Scale = 80 miles
Solid line by boat on the Rhine
Dotted line by horse or carriage

Herewith, dear Beatus, the full tragicomedy of my journey.[1] I left Basle, as you know, in a languid and enervated state, not having fully recovered my health despite a long stay at home, because it had been occupied with constant work. The boat trip was not disagreeable except that around midday the heat of the sun became oppressive. We dined at Breisach, but after a fashion that couldn't have been more disagreeable. The stench of the place was atrocious and the swarms of flies even worse. For half an hour we sat around the table, waiting for the people to bring out their food; and when it finally arrived, it was absolutely inedible; a gray mush, lumps of greasy meat, pieces of fish reheated for the sixth time—enough to turn your stomach. I didn't get to see Gallinarius. The man who reported he was suffering from a slight fever also added a choice tidbit; it seems that Minorite friar with whom I had quarrel over *haecitas*[2] managed to steal and pawn a holy church chalice. Now there's Scotist subtlety for you! Just before dark we were pushed off the boat into some icy little village: I didn't want to know its name, or if I knew it then to remember it now; I nearly perished there. I think there were more than sixty of us in one small overheated room, a ragtag collection of men from ten o'clock on; oh what a stench and what an uproar, especially after they got liquored up. And of course they had no sense of time, so the racket went all night.

In the morning while it was still dark, we were routed out of bed by the shouts of the boatmen. For my part, I'd had no sleep, and I got on the boat without any breakfast. We reached Strausbourg well before lunchtime, about the hour of nine; and there we were better received, especially with Schurer[3] supplying the wine. There were also some members of a literary society of which the other members soon arrived to greet me, but nobody more obligingly than Gerbel. Gebwiler and Rudolphingen stood treat for me, to greet me, which for them is no new practice. From there we set off on horseback for Speyer; on the way we saw not the least sign of soldiers, though rumor had spread frightful stories about them. My English horse gave out when we had barely reached Speyer; may the rascally smith who shod him so badly have both his ears pierced with red-hot nails! At Speyer I slipped away from the inn and betook myself to my Maternum[4] nearby. There the dean, a man of learning and humanity, detained me with his polite hospitality for two days; and there by chance I encountered Herman Busch.

From Speyer I took a carriage to Worms and from there to Mainz. As it happened, one of the Emperor's secretaries was in the same coach, a man named Ulrich Farnbul, which is to say Fernhill. Throughout the whole journey he took incredible pains to look out for me, and when we couldn't get into Mainz[5], he led me off "in the fullness of his knowledge" to the house of a certain canon; and then, on my departure, he took me down to the boat. Again the boatride was not disagreeable, since the weather was fine, though the sailors worked hard to make the trip longer than necessary. There was also a good deal of stink from the horses aboard. My kind companions on this first day were John Longicamianus, who used to teach at Louvain, and a certain lawyer friend of his. There was also a Westphalian, Doctor John, who was a canon of Saint Victor's outside Mainz—a most agreeable and jolly companion.

When we reached Boppard, where the boat had to pass a customs inspection, we passengers debarked and strolled along the bank when someone pointed me out to the customs agent: "there's the man." The agent was, if I'm not mistaken, a certain Christopher Cinincamius, in the vulgar tongue Eschenfelder. You wouldn't believe how the man carried on in his ecstasies. He takes us to his house, where on a table among various business papers lie some volumes of Erasmus. He declares himself overjoyed, he calls in his wife and children and all his friends. When the sailors start calling for us to return, he sends them a couple of bottles of wine, when they call again he sends them more, he promises that when the boat returns he will pass them duty-free, in gratitude for having brought such a man to him. From here as far as the juncture of the Moselle we were accompanied by Doctor John Flamming, prefect of the nunnery, a man of angelic purity, sane and sober judgment, and uncommon learning. At the juncture, Doctor Matthias, chancellor to the archbishop, carried us off to his house; though he is a young man, his manners are polished, his Latin excellent, and he is an accomplished lawyer. We had dinner at his house.

At Bonn, the canon left us, to avoid the city of Cologne;[6] I would rather have avoided it too, but my servant with the horses had preceded me there, and nobody

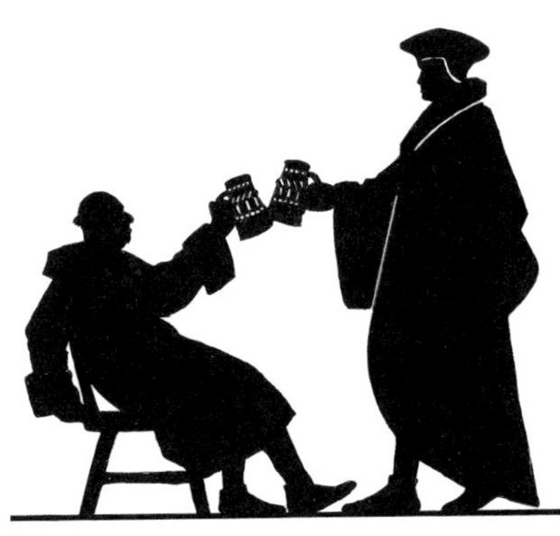

in the boat was confident that I could send a messenger to recall him; I was particularly doubtful about employing any of the sailors. So the next day we reached
Cologne before six o'clock of a Sunday morning under an already menacing sky.
Having reached the inn, I ordered the servants of the host to hire a shay and
prepare me a meal for ten o'clock. But the meal was put off so I could hear mass,
and nothing happened about the shay. I tried to get hold of a new horse, for my
own horses were useless. Nothing happened. Finally, I caught on; they were trying to keep me there. I promptly ordered my own horse saddled, loaded one of
my saddlebags on them, and left the other for the host to forward by boat. Then,
climbing on my limping nag, I set off toward the count of Neuenahr.[7] It was a five-
hour journey before I found him at Bedburg.

At this man's house I remained very comfortable for five days, enjoying so
much calm and leisure that I was able to carry out a good many revisions on my
manuscript—for I had brought with me part of my New Testament edition. I
only wish you were acquainted with this man, my dear Beatus! Young he is, but
of wisdom greater than years generally bring; a man of few words, but as Homer
says of Menelaos, "clear and judicious," learned without ostentation and not just
in one narrow subject, utterly frank, and a warm, genial friend. Now I felt vigor-
ous, even a bit robust, and soon I looked forward to greeting, in the fullness of
my health, the bishop of Liège, and to appearing in fine fettle among my friends
in Brabant.[8] What merry dinners, what brave compliments, what rich conversa-
tions I promised myself! I even thought, if the autumn proved fine, of going to
England and accepting there what the king has so often offered me. But oh, the
foolish hopes of mortal men! oh the sudden and unexpected twists of human
affairs! From all these dreams of felicity I was tumbled abruptly into the pit of
misfortune.

My shay was to be ready next morning. The count, unwilling to say his good-
byes the night before, promised to come and see me off in the morning before
I left. That night a savage windstorm blew up, which had made itself felt even

the day before. I rose nonetheless just after midnight, having certain things to communicate to the count. When seven o'clock came, and the count had not yet appeared, I sent a servant to wake him up. He came, and in his usual gentle way asked whether under such inclement conditions I was still determined to leave; he said he feared for my safety. At that point, my Beatus, some god, I know not which, or some evil demon, took away, not half my mind, as Hesiod says,[9] but the whole thing; for half my mind was already missing when I decided to go to Cologne. And I only wish that he had warned me, as his friend, more sharply, or that I had listened more submissively to his concerned, and perfectly accurate, warnings. But the power of fate was on me; what else is there to say? I got into the uncovered shay, the wind blowing

> As from the high peaks it descends
> To rend the trembling oaks.[10]

It was a south wind, laden with nothing but pure pestilence. I tried to huddle under my robes, but the wind in its violence drove right through them. Showers of rain swept down on me from the dark sky, more pestilent even than the wind. I reached Aix exhausted by the bumping of the shay, which rattled over the cobblestone roads so painfully that I would rather have been sitting on a horse, however lame he was. In Aix a certain canon, whom the count had recommended as my guardian, dragged me out of my inn to the house of the precentor. There, as usual, several canons were deep in drink. My appetite had been sharpened by a very light lunch; but they had nothing to eat except some carp, and it was cold. I ate it. The drinking went on till late at night. I excused myself on the ground that I'd had very little sleep the night before, and went to bed.

Next morning, I was taken to the house of the vice-provost, for it was his turn to entertain visitors. Here, since there was no manner of fresh fish except eel (doubtless the storm was to blame, since as a rule he is said to set a magnificent table), I had to make do with that dried fish which the Germans call, after the stick with which it is pulped, *stockfish*. Ordinarily, I find it palatable; but a good part of this was practically raw. After lunch, since the weather was still threatening, I went back to my inn, and ordered a fire to be lit in my room. The canon, who was a man of good heart, sat with me for about an hour and a half, making conversation. But all the while, my stomach was acting up; and when it continued in turmoil, I sent him away, went to the latrine, and emptied my bowels. That still brought no relief, so I stuck my finger down my throat again and again, until finally that raw fish came up, but nothing else. Lying down after my fit of vomiting, I didn't so much sleep as doze, but without pain either of head or body; then, having arranged with the driver to bring up my bag, I found myself invited to another nocturnal drinking-bout. I made excuses, but unsuccessfully.

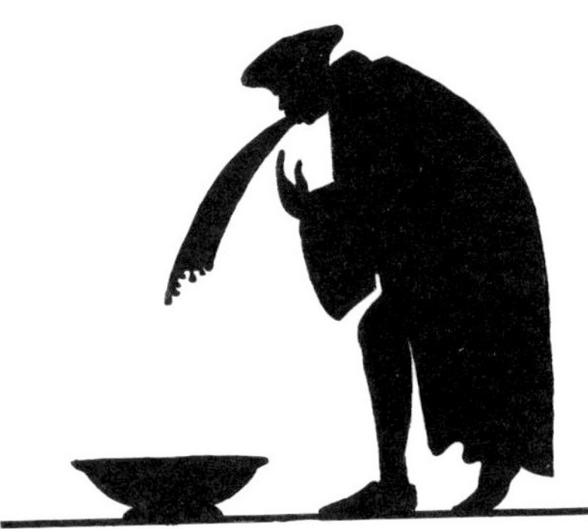

I knew that my stomach could endure nothing but warm broth. For the same thing happened one night in Basle, when, not realizing that my stomach could would be terribly distressed by putting slimy food into it, I raised it to fury; a month passed after that before my stomach could accept regular food again. The meal was splendid that night, but it wasn't for me. When I had soothed my stomach with a bit of broth, I went home—for they had me sleeping in the precentor's house. As I left the party, my empty body shivered violently under the cold night sky. It was a long night.

Next morning I breakfasted on a bit of warm beer and a few crusts of bread, then mounted my lame and ailing horse; more ungainly riding you never saw. By now I was so distressed as to be more fit for a bed than a saddle. But there's no part of the world more wretched, uncouth, or disagreeable than this, such is the degradation of the people. My only thought was to get away. Fear of robbers, who flourish in these parts, was wholly dispelled by the pains of my illness.

Back in Basle, I used sometimes to scratch parts of my groin as a way of stimulating my bowels and once, scratching particularly hard, my nail made a little break in the skin inside my left leg. The same thing happened on my right thigh, but without causing any pain or infection. The sore on my left leg got a little irritated on my two-day ride from Strasbourg to Speyer, but I still felt it only when I sat on it heavily. My most recent horseback ride had inflamed this sore spot even further, since that was where I pressed hardest on the saddle; the whole area was tender. In addition, the sore on my right leg swelled up a little, like an abscess under the skin, but still without pain. On the top of my left leg a further hard swelling developed, but again without pain and without infection. When I rode a horse, these parts were not well protected from the wind.

After a trip of about sixteen miles, I reached Maastricht, where after sipping some more broth to keep my stomach warm, I took once more to horse, and reached Tongres; the distance was about twelve miles. This last stage was by far the most painful to me. The irregular gait of the horse caused me great pain about my kid-

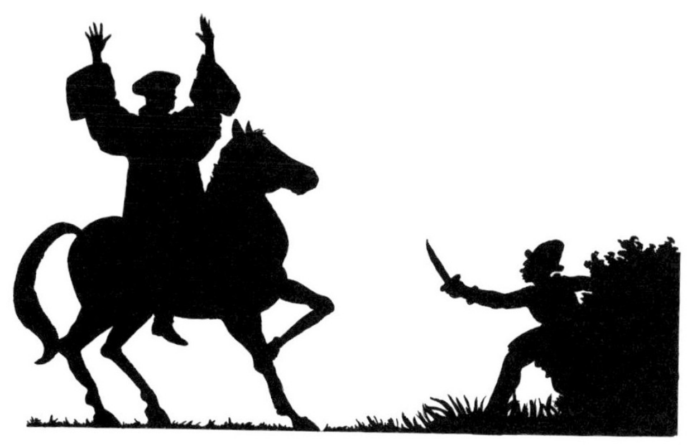

neys, and I thought I might get along more comfortably on foot; but I feared to work up a sweat and there was danger lest night overtake us in the open country. And so, suffering from incredible pains throughout my body but especially in the kidneys and liver, I got to Tongres. At this point, what with hunger and weariness, every muscle in my body was unstrung; I couldn't either stand or walk steadily. But with my tongue—which was still operative—I covered up the extent of my debility, soothed my stomach with a bit of broth, and went to bed.

Next day I ordered a covered shay. My plan was to ride a horse where the road was paved with stones, until I got to a smoother dirt road. I saddled the bigger horse because he was more sure-footed on cobblestones. But hardly was I mounted in the chill morning air than my sight failed, everything went black. I called for a cloak, but promptly fainted away. They revived me by rubbing my arms and legs. With the help of several bystanders, my servant John held me on the horse and brought me to my senses. When I had recovered a little, I got into the shay. Somewhat later, I felt the need to move my bowels; I got out, did my business, and shortly felt some color return to my face and a certain liveliness to my limbs. By now we were near the town of Saint Trond. Once more I mounted the horse, lest, being carried in a shay, I might seem an invalid. As evening fell, I suffered once again from nausea, but there was no more fainting. I offered the driver of the shay a double fee to drive me next day as far as Tirlemont: it's a town about twenty-four miles from Tongres. He accepted the offer. Here a fellow traveler whom I knew told me how hurt the bishop of Liège had been at my leaving for Basle without paying him a courtesy call.[11] I took a little broth for my stomach, and went to bed. The night was extremely painful, especially because of the sore on my left leg; it was now infected and covered with a big scab. But here by good luck I was able to take a stage coach on its way to Louvain (about twenty miles away),[12] and I flung myself into it. The trip was horribly, almost unbearably, painful; but at last, about seven o'clock of that day, we reached Louvain.

I was in no mood to seek my own quarters because I suspected they were icy cold, and also because I didn't want to be responsible—if rumors of the plague got about—for disrupting the work of the college. So I turned aside to the house of Theodoric the printer.[13] He is such a good friend that, if I had my way, I could be happy with his acquaintance alone. That night, during my sleep, the biggest of my boils burst, and the pain diminished. Next day I went to the doctor, who applied poultices. Now a third sore broke out on my back; it had been made by a servant at Tongres when he was trying to relieve the pain of my kidneys, and in rubbing my back with oil of roses dug too deeply into my ribs with his horny finger. Afterwards this sore began to fester, another swelling appeared, moving around in the neighborhood of my right nipple; but it didn't come to a head, and after a while it slowly disappeared of its own accord. As the doctor departed, he secretly told Theodoric and his servant that I had the plague, that he would send over more poultices, but would not return himself to look after me. I sent a urine specimen to the doctors, they said it showed no evidence of sickness; I consult other doctors, they say the same thing. I call in a Jewish doctor, he says on the evidence of the specimen my body is just as healthy as his. When the original doctor did not return for a couple of days, I asked Theodoric what was the matter. He made some vague excuse, but I suspected the truth. "What!" I said, "does he think it's the plague?" "That's it," he told me; "he says confidently that there are three plague sores." I laughed heartily, and put all thoughts of the plague out of my mind.

After a couple of days the father of the original doctor shows up, looks me over, and reaches the same conclusion; he tells me to my face that I have the plague. I summon on the side another physician of great reputation. He looks me over, and as he's a blunt man, says, "I wouldn't hesitate to get in bed with you; and if you were a woman, we could have fun together." The Jew agrees with him. Finally, I went to the very best doctor in Louvain—for in fact good doctors are pretty scarce here. I asked if the urine specimen showed anything bad; he said no. I told him the story of my sores, showing in various ways that they couldn't be plague sores. They weren't new sores, they hadn't appeared of their

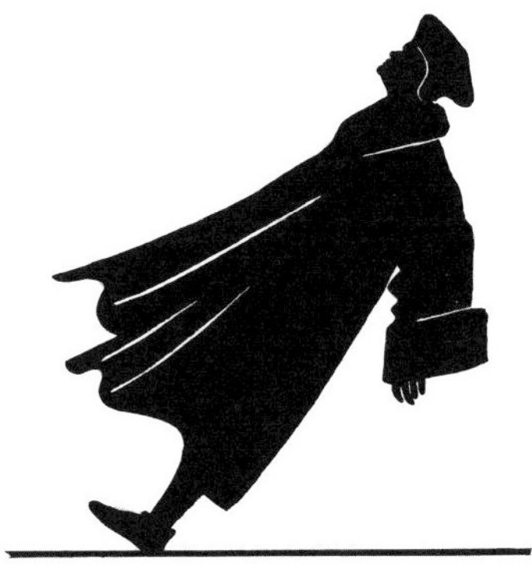

own accord. At the beginning the sores moved about, the one on my left thigh always did so. I had no fever, no particular headache except from being constantly shaken about; I wasn't unusually sleepy, and my palate always felt clean. The vomiting wasn't spontaneous, I provoked it myself and I threw up nothing but that fish. Once free of that, my stomach recovered; that I rejected food for a time is simply a special mannerism of mine. The urine showed no signs of the plague. Most of this discourse he listened to bravely enough; but whenever I mentioned my sores and boils, I felt the man getting uneasy. I gave him a gold crown, and he promised to return after lunch; but instead, having been terrified by my account, he sent his servant. I kicked him out, and, being thoroughly sick of doctors, commended myself to Christ as my physician.

Within three days my stomach was back to normal after I had drunk a bowl of chicken soup and a bottle of wine from Beaune. I promptly returned to my studies, working over some passages in my New Testament that needed filling out. After seventeen days my wounds gave off some black and putrid matter, as the doctors had predicted would happen. The swelling on my left thigh grew even larger, though without any pain, but it caused me some worry. Then a ridiculous suspicion entered my mind—I hope it's wrong—that this infection came from contact with my horse. For I often slapped barehanded at the flies that settled on him, and then proceeded to touch these parts of my body, either when urinating or when getting dressed. But my new physician calmly advises me to be secure of mind. Now the swelling is going down and getting softer, but it doesn't change its position. The sores are all out of danger, that lump on my right breast having vanished of its own accord.

After recuperating for almost four weeks at Theodoric's house, I returned to my own quarters. During that time I had been so weak that I went out only once to hear mass. If it was the plague, I overcame it by determination, by other distractions, and by strength of mind, for very often the worst part of a disease is the thought of it. From the day of my return I decreed that nobody should come near me unless summoned by name, since I didn't want anyone to be frightened or to have his kindness turned to his disadvantage. Nevertheless, Dorp came to see me first of all, and then Ath. Mark Laurin and Pascal Bersel, who stopped by every day, relieved me during much of my illness with their delightful conversation.

My dear Beatus, who would suppose this thin little body of mine, delicate to begin with and now worn out with age, after going through the pains of so many journeys and the drudgery of so much study, would be able to survive so much sickness? You know how hard I worked at Basle recently, and not just off and on. I had a premonition that this year would be fatal for me; and in fact one trouble succeeded another, each more serious than its predecessor. When the illness was at its height, I was not much disturbed, either by a yearning for life or by a fear of death. My entire trust was in Christ alone, of whom I asked only that he give me whatever fate he thought best. In my youth, as I recall, I used to shudder at the very name of death. At least I have profited from the passing years in fearing death less and in estimating human happiness less in terms of longevity. Already I have passed my fiftieth year; since so few out of so many reach that stage, it's only right for me to ask if I haven't already lived long enough. Besides, if this enters in, I've already prepared the monument by which posterity can know I existed. And perhaps, to quote the poets, when heard from the funeral pyre the voices of envy grow still while glory sounds more loudly.[14] Though, of course, it's no part of the Christian spirit to care for earthly glory; quite enough if I experience that supreme glory of rendering myself acceptable to Christ. Farewell, my dear Beatus. You will learn the sequel from my letter to Capito.[15]

From Louvain, 1518

Notes

1. As the crow flies, the distance from Basle in Switzerland to Louvain in Belgium is about 260 miles; when Erasmus undertook this journey in the fall of 1518, he elected to follow the great waterway of the Rhine to cover much of the distance. Then from Cologne to Louvain, a scant hundred miles or so, he could proceed by horse or light carriage. How he made out, his letter describes. It was addressed to his good friend and associate Beatus Rhenanus (who acquired his last name because his father came from Rheinau and his first name from a cheery disposition). Rhenanus had worked alongside Erasmus in John Froben's Basle printing house.

The towns at which the traveling scholar stopped are indicated on an outline map (p. 26); among the people he encountered—many of them casual acquaintances of his or of Rhenanus—it has seemed desirable to annotate only the most prominent.

2. Literally, "thisness"; the scholastic word for the individuating essence that defines the special reality of an object. Erasmus objected to the word not only as barbarous Latin but as pretentiously obscure.

3. Schurer, a printer at Strasbourg, had been an employer of Beatus Rhenanus. Note how Erasmus, leaving the house of Froben at Basle, could rely on a network of printers and publishers stretching across Europe, for the comforts (and sometimes the necessities) of existence.

4. Maternum: perhaps the cathedral church at Speyer, perhaps an Augustinian monastery in the neighborhood; Erasmus still maintained contact with his old order.

5. Either because there was no room at the inn or for fear of the plague, prevalent that fall in many cities of Germany.

6. Cologne was definitely hard hit by the plague.

7. Herman, count of Neuenahr (1492–1530).

8. Braabant is a district of southern Holland and northern Belgium where Erasmus had spent much of his youth. Through his various agents, Henry VII held out many inducements for Erasmus to settle in England—so various and so vague that it's hard to know which ones he has in mind here.

9. Hesiod, "The Shield of Hercules" 149.

10. Horace, *Epodes* 10.

11. The complaint dates back four months, to May of 1518, when Erasmus left Louvain for Basle.

12. It's doubtful whether the last stage of Erasmus' trip took him from Tirlemont or from Saint Trond to Louvain. Dates and distances are not altogether distinct in his account.

13. Theodoric Martinus, another in the network of Erasmus' printer friends. To take in a man who might be suffering from the plague was a heroic act.

14. Ovid, *Amores* 1.15.39.

15. Wolfgang Capito (1478–1541); Allen reprints Erasmus' letter to him as his no. 877.

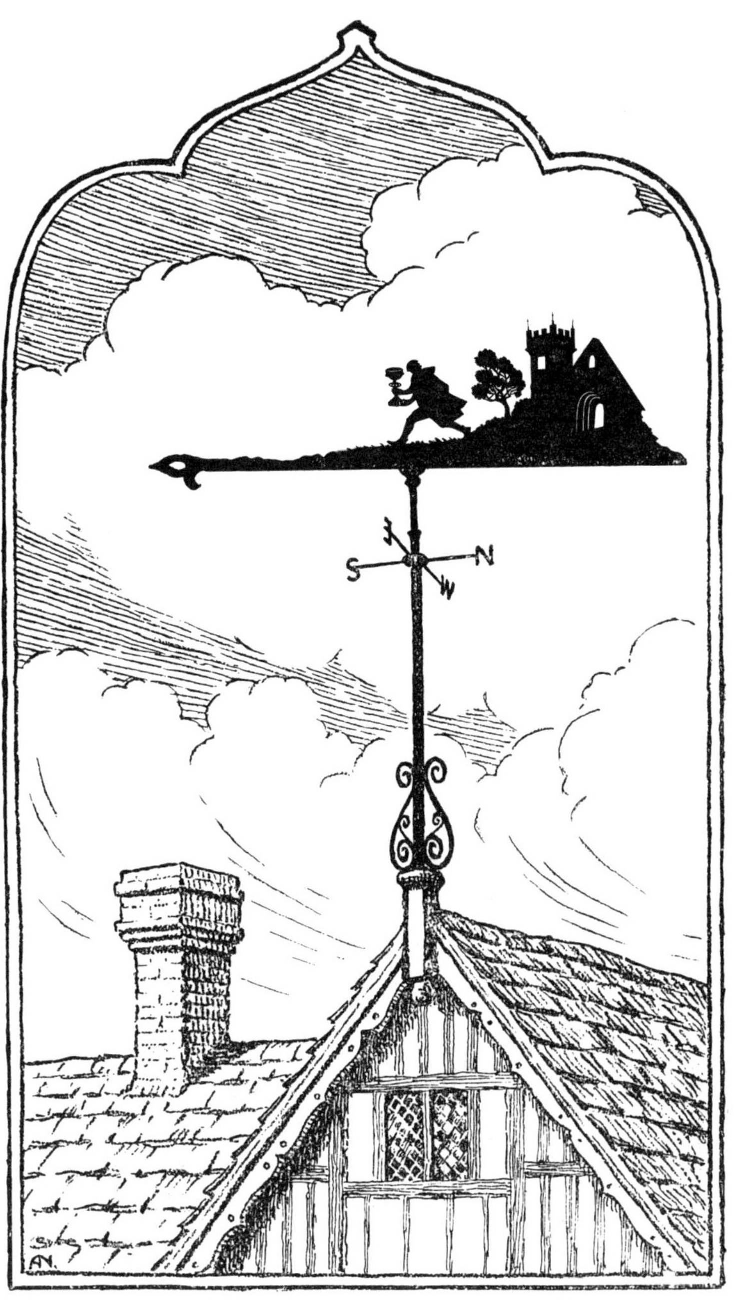

S
N
W

A BRIEF HISTORY OF ENGLISH WEATHERVANES
A. Needham, F.R.S.A., A.M.C.

A definition, printed in the *Encyclopaedia Britannica*, gives no indication of the extremely interesting examples of craftwork in iron and copper that are revealed by the study of English weathervanes.

"Vane (formerly spelt 'fane,' i.e., pennon, flag); c.f. Ger., Fahne; Du., Vaan; Fr., Girouette; Ital., Banderuola; Ger., Wetterfahne (the weathercock on a steeple). Vanes seem in early times to have been of various forms as dragons, &c.; but in the Tudor period the favourite design was a beast or bird sitting on a slender pedestal and carrying an upright rod, on which a thin plate of metal is hung like a flag, ornamented in various ways," see Fig. 7, Plate XXVI.

The origin of weathervanes is lost in the dim past. It may be that smoke first drew primitive man's attention to the changing direction of the wind. When he lit a fire at the mouth of his cave to protect his family from the attacks of wild beasts he would notice that, on some days, his dwelling would be unpleasantly filled with smoke, while at other times the smoke drifted away from the cave. Then he would come to learn, when hunting animals for food and clothing, that it was necessary to approach his prey from the windward side so that the animal should not pick up his scent and thus be on the alert.

During the time the Romans occupied Britain they used smoke for signalling in the daytime (e.g., from the Roman lighthouse at Dover) and from the forts of the Saxon shore, and the smoke would serve equally to indicate the direction of the wind.

Small flags, blown in various directions by changing winds may have suggested the making and use of weathervanes. Evidence of the very early use of flags exists, a few examples are given below, with drawings on Plate I. As will be seen from the illustrations in this book, weathervanes have, for centuries, been made in flag-like shapes.

Carvings and paintings, supplemented by ancient writings, show that companies of the Egyptian army carried staves having such emblems as sacred animals, boats, figures, etc., representing "Nomes" or districts. These staves were frequently ornamented below the emblem with streamers. Fig. 1, Plate I, is an illustration of one such staff from a bas-relief on the Abydos Temple of Seti I (c. 1300 B.C., XIXth Dynasty). When the bearers carried these staves, with the streamers flowing in the wind, the archers discharging their arrows, and having to take into consideration the direction and velocity of the wind would, no doubt, find the streamers of use as indicators.

Part of the facade of the temple of Luxor (restored by Ch. Chipiez) shows, in Fig. 2, Plate I, a pole with streamers serving as decoration, which could also play their part as wind direction indicators. The temple was begun under Amenhotep III, c. 1400 B.C.

Fig. 5, Plate I, shows the spear, with small flag attached, carried by Grecian soldiers as depicted on the famous "Warrior Vase" (Mycenæan Age in Greece, 1600–1100 B.C.). It may be the origin of the pennons on the lances of Mediæval knights.

The drawing (from a restoration after Thiersch) in Fig. 3, Plate I, shows the upper part of the ancient Pharos (lighthouse), built under Ptolemy II, about 260 B.C., and accounted one of the seven wonders of the world. It stood on the island of Pharos at the entrance to the harbour of Alexandria. It appears to have two long streamers which would show mariners the direction of the wind.

Livy (59 B.C.–A.D. 17) describes the Vexillum, the standard of the cavalry of the ancient Roman army, as a square piece of cloth fastened to a piece of wood fixed crosswise at the end of a spear.

A reconstruction of the Circus Maximus (4th century) shows tall poles having streamers attached to them, see Fig. 12, Plate I.

Illustrations of ships in the years B.C. do not indicate that flags were used on them, but Fig. 10, Plate I, a drawing from a Boeotian fibula, made of bronze, and now in the British Museum, shows a Greek boat (about 8th century) which carries a banner-like flag at the top of the mast, so that it is possible that flags on ships were used in earlier years.

Figs. 6, 8, and 9, Plate I, illustrate pennons on the lances of knights of the 11th century as seen on the Bayeux Tapestry. A banner on the lance of Simon de Montfort, c. 1231, is shown in Fig. 15, Plate I, while in Fig. 6, is the pennon on the lance of St. John D'Abernon, 1277, shown on the "brass" in Stoke D'Abernon Church, Surrey, stated to be the earliest specimen of a "brass" in England.

That the suggestions as to the origin weathervanes mentioned earlier, are not unreasonable, is indicated by the statement in the recent issue of the Air Ministry's *Meteorological Observers' Handbook,* to the effect that, in the absence of a vane, a good wind indicator is furnished by a streamer (a long narrow flag) attached to a tall flag-staff in an open situation; and the direction of smoke should be noted also.

Whatever it was that suggested the making and erecting of weathervanes, they have been, and still continue to be, most useful to mankind. Even in these times when, through the British Broadcasting service, weather reports are regularly sent out, they are general ones covering wide areas, and local winds may vary in direction, which would be shown by the vanes on nearby buildings.

Vitruvius, *De Architectura,* Lib. I.C.ij, refers to what may have been the earliest weathervane, surmounting "The Horologion," of Andronicus Cyrrhestes (the so-called "Tower of the Winds" in Athens), c. 50 B.C.

A translation reads: ". . . they put also a golden Triton holding a rod in its right hand and it is constructed in such a way that it is turned by the wind in such a manner that it always stays against the wind, holding the rod as an indication above the image of the blowing wind." Fig. 4, Plate I, is from a reconstruction of the Triton on top of the tower, by J. C. Basing, sculptor; for the vane is now missing. (Note. — Triton. In Greek mythology, a minor sea diety, son of Poseidon, represented as part man, part fish).

The "Tower of Winds" is an octagonal building with a frieze representing the eight winds (N., N.E., E., S.E., S., S.W., W., N.W.). One of these figures, "Kaikias" (shield full of hail), signifying the north east wind, is shown in Fig. 7, Plate I. (Radcliffe Observatory, built at Oxford in the 18th century, has a tower based on the "Tower of Winds," and having the eight sculptured figures representing the winds).

There is little indication of other very early weathervanes except, it is reported, that Rome had a somewhat similar building to the "Tower of Winds," and that in the 4th century a female figure turned in the wind over a building in Constantinople. An illustration in the *History of Skylitzes* (from Schlumberger, *L'épopée byzantine,* Hachette), depicts the East Roman Empress Zoe (who died A.D. 1050) leaving the church of S. Sophia, Constantinople, and entering her Palace. On the church is shown a weathercock with a cross above it. The cock, like all other Christian symbols, was probably eliminated by the Turks when they converted the church into a mosque in 1543, or it may only have existed in the artist's imagination. In spite of the paucity of evidence it must not be assumed that other vanes were not in use during this early period. It may be possible that the Romans, during their occupation of Britain, used weathervanes here.

If one peruses the many literary references in the past, it can be appreciated that weathervanes were considered of much interest and importance. A few of these notes are given in the following extracts, with dates and translations where necessary.

R. K. Gordon in *Anglo-Saxon Poetry,* gives a quaint 8th century description (an Old English idea of a riddle), the answer in this case being a "weathercock."

"I am puff-breasted, swollen necked. I have a head and lofty tail, eyes and ears and one foot, a back and hard beak, a high neck and two sides, a rod in the middle, a dwelling above man, I endure misery when he who stirs the forest moves me; and torrents beat down upon me in my station, the hard hail and rime; and frost comes down and snow falls on me pierced through the stomach and I . . ." (Description is incomplete). Note: Shakespeare makes *King Lear* (Act III, Scene II) defiantly exclaim:

"Blow, winds, and crack our cheeks! rage! blow!
Your cataracts and hurricanoes, spout
Till you have drenched our steeples, drown'd the cocks!

A contemporary drawing in the 10th century *Benedictional of St. Ethelwold* shows the weathercock on the tower of Winchester Cathedral, see Fig. 11, Plate I.

A part of the Bayeux Tapestry, which is over 800 years old, shows a man, with a weathercock in his hand, about to mount the roof of Westminster Abbey (dedicated to St. Peter), built during the time of Edward the Confessor, and consecrated in 1065. Fig. 16, Plate I, shows the portion of the Tapestry referred to.

Memorials of Canterbury Cathedral, by C. E. Woodruff and W. Danks, contains a reference to the "guilded seraph on the top of Canterbury Cathedral." This was probably a weathervane. No date is given, but a 12th-century drawing shows, over the west end turrets of Canterbury Cathedral, two weathercocks.

c. 1233. Fig 13, Plate I, is a copy of part of an engraving depicting a weathercock on the tower of a hospital at Oxford, built by Henry III (Ms. Roy, 14c, vii).

In the 13th century a royal licence was required for the use of weathervanes, and these were restricted to the nobility. Small pennons were attached to the head of the lance and borne by a knight, sometimes having his cognizance upon it; see Figs. 6, 8 and 9, Plate I. It was usual in battle, to grant to the first knight to plant his pennon on the walls of a besieged town or castle, the Royal right to fix upon the highest part of his own castle or stronghold, his vane, emblazoned with his bearing or crest. Probably the primary object of these vanes was to display the arms of the knight; showing the direction of the wind being of secondary importance.

c. 1300 Neckham. *De Utensilibus* (i.e., about utensils), quoted in Wright's *Old English Vocabularies,* has a reference to a weathercock: "Ventilogium, Veder-coc."

c. 1307. In the *Cottonian MS Nero* DII, in the British Museum, a large weathercock is shown on the spire of St. Paul's Cathedral.

c. 1340. *The Ayen-bite of Inwit* (The Again-bite of the Inner Knowledge), by Richard Rolle, of Hampole, contains some words, the approximate translation being: "Therefore they beeth as the weathercock that is upon the steeple, that himself turns with each wind."

1365. In *Exch. K.R. Accts.* 462, 23 is stated that, in A.D. 1365, a weathervane was set up on the great tower of Dover Castle which was helpful to navigators of ships.

c. 1400. "Against women unconstant" is the title of a balade — a short poem of three seven-lined stanzas, ascribed to Chaucer, which includes the following: "But, as a wedercok that turneth his face with every wind, yet fare, and that is sene."

c. 1425. *Parochial Antiquities,*Vol. II, Kennet. "With two wind-readers, namely vanes of tin bought ———— to be put on each end of the said dormitory." (i.e. on the gables).

1479–1481. From the records of St. Mary-at-Hill Church, London. "Item for mendyng of the vane of the steple."

c. 1480. "Testament of Cresseid," a poem by Robert Henryson, a Scottish poet. The poem is a sequel to Chaucer's "Troilus and Cressida." (Note. — It is called a Testament be-cause it contains her dying speech at the end). The part relating to a weathercock reads: —

> "Thairfoir I reidze tak a ze find,
> For they are sad as weddercock in wind."
> (15th century Scottish dialect).

An approximate translation is: —

> "Therefore I advise ye take them as ye find,
> For they are as fixed as a weathercock in the wind."

c. 1483. A quotation from Caxton. "Be not like ne semblable the tortuse ne the crane which wynde their hede here and there as a vane." (Note.—"ne," i.e., nor).

In Henry the Seventh's time, a poet in *Tower of Doctrine* gives the following: —

"The little turrets with ymages of golde about was set, which with the wynde aye moved."

Fig. 14, Plate I, shows part of a building in an illustration from *Artillery in Action,* temp. Henry VIII, from an English treatise on artillery; MS. Cott. Vesp. A xvii (British Museum). On top of the building is a weathervane which appears to be in the form of some kind of dragon.

c. 1515. *Archaeologia X,* 85, contains an account of the erection of a weathercock on Louth church steeple in the presence of priests who sang the Te Deum Laudamus. Afterwards the bells were rung, and bread and ale was distributed to the people.

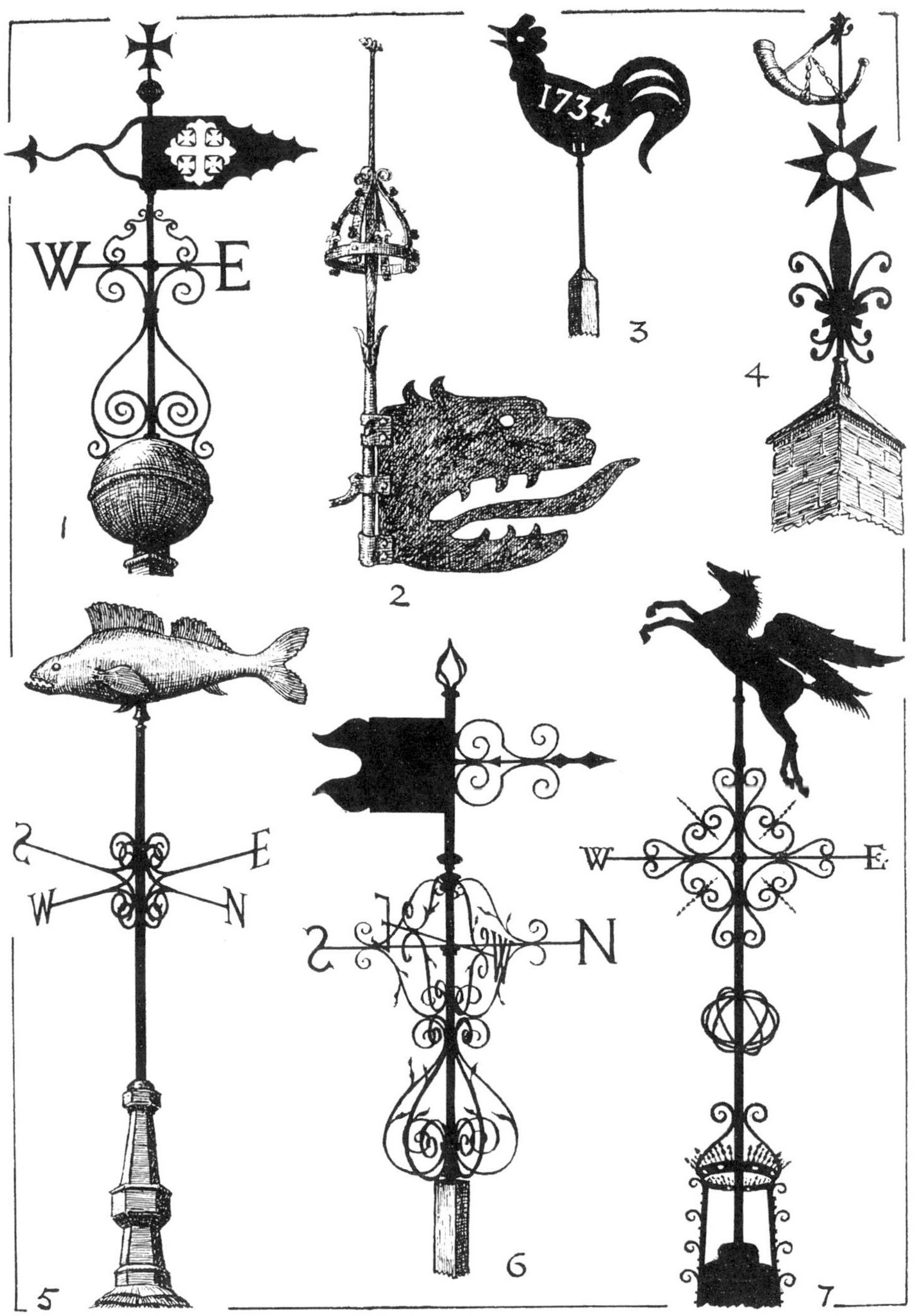

WEATHERVANES ON PUBLIC BUILDINGS

c. 1546. *Church Goods (in the Diocese of) York* (a publication of the Surtees Society). "The said steple havyng a whether cokke thereuppon all gylt."

c. 1548. Hall. *Chronicles of Henry VIII.* "Over the gates wer arches with towers embattailed, set with vanes and scutchions of the armes of the Emperor and the Kyng."

1597. In *The Wisdom of Solomon Paraphrased,* by T. Middleton, is the following: — "Like a vane turn'd with every blast."

1606. A record in the Spalding Club, Aberdeen Burch, reads: — "16th April 1606. David Anderstone, maister of Kirk wark to send brazen cok of the stepill of Sanct Nicolas Parish Kirk this burght of Flanderis to be medit thair and owergilt and to be erectit and set vp vpon the hicht of the said stepill."

1661. In the records of All Saints' Church, Hereford, 1661. "To John Williams, plasterer, for pulling downe and putting up the whether cocke." (This probably refers to doing the necessary repairs, or perhaps to the periodical cleaning of the bearing to ensure that the weathercock turned in the wind).

1662. The Vicar of Bray, mentioned by Thomas Fuller in his *History of the Worthies of England,* was likened to a weathercock because of his frequent change of opinions.

The celebrated Vicar lived in the reigns of Henry VIII, Edward VI, Queen Mary and Queen Elizabeth. In order to retain his Office he was, in turn, a Papist, then a Protestant, and again a Papist and afterwards a Protestant.

Part of a well-known song about the Vicar reads: —

> "For this is law I will maintain
> Until my dying day, Sir,
> That whatsoever King doth reign
> I'll be the Vicar of Bray, Sir."

1683. D.A. in *Art of Converse.* "Some are as changeable as weathercocks in their humours."

1833. L. Ritchie. *Wand Loire.* "The Duc de Choiseul —— consoled himself by setting up the head of Voltaire as a weathercock."

c. 1864. "Aylmer's Field," a poem by Tennyson, includes the following: — "Whose blazing wyvern weathercocked the spire."

1867. H. Latham. *Black and White.* "The most conspicuous weathercock in the town is a golden trumpet on the spire of one of the churches."

Many more literary references to weathervanes could be quoted.

Figs. 2 and 5, Plate IV, show what are reputed to be the oldest English weathercock and weathervane still in use.

A number of vanes have, as part of their design, the date when they were made; but it must not be assumed that these vanes are, in every case, the original ones. Evidence shows, that some having been blown down and broken, copies of the original vanes were made and erected in the place of the damaged one.

Early weathervanes in this country were of a banner-like form without a pointer, see Fig. 5, Plate IV, and Figs. 6 and 7, Plate XXVI. It is not possible to state when pointers first came into general use. A vane, dated 1577, see Fig 1, Plate XXVI, is shown with a pointer, as are some 17th-century ones, see Plates IV, V and XI.

Good examples of vanes, which might otherwise have been lost when buildings were pulled down, have been saved by some museum authorities (including the Victoria and Albert, London), who thought the vanes were worth preserving and exhibiting, see Figs. 2 and 6, Plate XI, Figs. 13 and 14, Plate XII, and Fig. 7, Plate XVI.

Lighthouse keepers, having to write weather records, are provided with weathervanes fitted with interior dials, somewhat similar to the Greenwich Observatory one, see Plate II.

Few people realise that there are still in position, in some parts of this country, very old telegraph poles with weathervanes on top of them, see Fig. 16, Plate XIII.

There are other vanes, which, while they cannot strictly be termed weathervanes, are operated by the wind, and are so constructed that they turn the object they are fixed upon until they are in the most favourable position for their purpose, see Plate XIX, Figs. 21, 22, 26, 27, 28, and Plate XXXVII, Fig. 79.

Some modern weathervane designs in the form of representations of human figures, animals, etc., can be seen painted in naturalistic colours which rarely add to their artistic appearance, and, unless the vanes are on a low building, the colour is not easily seen. There are, however, cases in which colour is an advantage, such as those depicting Dalmatian dogs, see Plate XXIII, Fig. 51, or when a design shows a special breed of cow and colour would make it easier to identify the breed.

That the colouring of weathervanes is not a modern innovation can be seen by the following extract: — *Select. Rec. Oxford* (W H. Turner). "For . . . coloring the beasts and the vanes and the Quenes arms . . . with colors and oyles."

Sir W. St. J. Hope in *Windsor Castle*, A.D. 1352, refers to a vane on the Hall at Windsor which was painted with the King's Arms.

Gilded weathervanes have a very picturesque appearance, showing flashes of bright gold against a blue sky as they turn in the wind. This aspect is referred to by Scott, in *Woodstock*, Vol. II (A.D. 1826), "One or two . . . venerable turrets, bearing each its own vane of rare device glittering in the sun;" and also by L. Morris, in *Ode of Life* (A.D. 1880), "The old grey church, with the tall spire, whose vane the sun sets fire."

Weathervanes constructed of copper turn a lovely green colour which is enhanced when the sun shines on them. This colour, when copper is exposed to the atmosphere, is caused by the formation of basic copper carbonate from the reaction of the copper, moisture and carbon di-oxide. The colour varies, due to environment; in town air, copper sulphate is a constituent, while by the sea, copper sulphide is produced.

This brief survey is sufficient to indicate that the use of weathervanes in this country has continued for many centuries, and their use shows little sign of waning popularity.

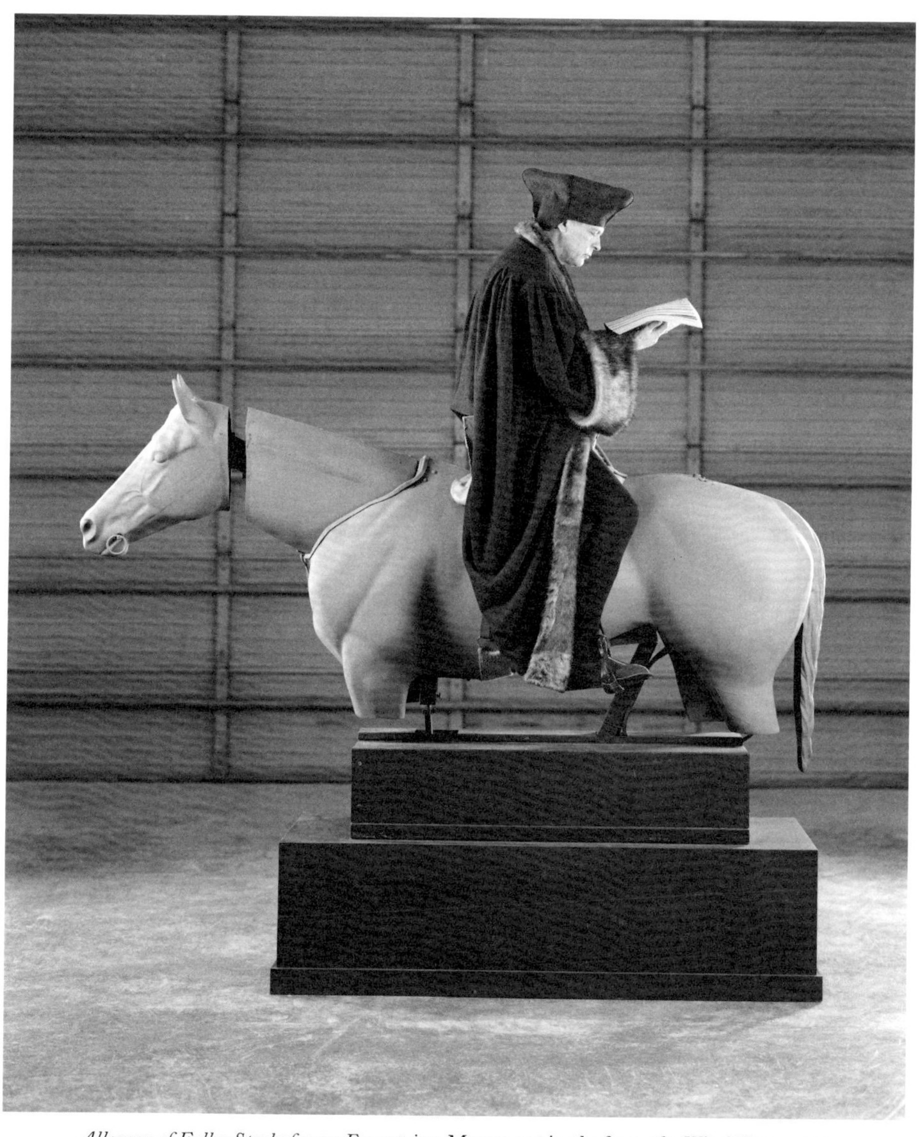

Allegory of Folly: Study for an Equestrian Monument in the form of a Wind Vane, 2005
Rodney Graham

SELECTED LIST OF
EQUESTRIAN STATUES IN ENGLAND
Compiled by Valentine Blacque and Ariel Thornycroft Dill

BEDFORDSHIRE:
Equestrian Statue Group, Silsoe

BUCKINGHAMSHIRE:
George I, Stowe, Aylesbury Vale
Frederick Prince of Wales, Hartwell House, Aylesbury Vale

CHESHIRE:
Equestrian Statue, Stable Yard, Chester
Equestrian Statue, Central Terrace, Chester
Hugh Lupus, by George Frederick Watts, Eccleston
Stapleton Cotton Viscount Combermere, by Carlo Marochetti, Chester Castle, Chester

BERKSHIRE:
Prince Albert, by Joseph E. Boehm, Windsor
Charles I, by Strado, Windsor
George III, by Sir Richard Westmacott, Windsor
James II, Windsor

DEVON:
Gen. Sir Redvers Buller, New North Road, Exeter

DURHAM:
Third Marquis of Londonderry, by Monti, Market Place, Durham

EAST MIDLANDS:
Bonnie Prince Charlie, Derby

GLOUCESTERSHIRE:
Emperor Nerva, Gloucester
John Wesley, Broadmead, Bristol
William III, Queen Square, by J. M. Rysbrack, Queen Square, Bristol

HAMPSHIRE:
Duke of Wellington, by R. Wyatt, Aldershot
George I, Basingstoke and Deane
Wellington Monument, Aldershot
William III, The Square, Petersfield

(continued on back cover)

ACKNOWLEDGEMENTS

With gratitude and great appreciation to Laura Lindgren for the design of this book and to Jason Burch for all of his help in realizing this project. With special thanks to Rodney Graham and to Scott Livingstone and Shannon Oksanen at the Rodney Graham studio; to Iwona Blazwick, Anthony Spira, and Candy Stobbs at the Whitechapel Gallery; to John Slyce and family in London; to Donald Young and Emily Letourneau at the Donald Young Gallery; to Ariel Thornycroft Dill, Catherine Ecclestone, Emily Helck, and Marlo Kovach at the Christine Burgin Gallery/William Wegman studio; to Robert Kleyn and the Robert Kleyn Studio, Vancouver and also to Pamela Barr, Zoe and Halla Beloff, Wojciech Blaszczyk, Paulette Chigar, Suzanne Salinetti, and Neil Wedman.

Design: Laura Lindgren
Printing: The Studley Press

British Weathervanes by R. Graham
copyright © 2009 Rodney Graham and Christine Burgin

ISBN: 978-0-692-00218-6

CREDITS

Page 6: Photo-Tint by James Akerman. Reproduced courtesy Tower Hamlets Local History Library and Archives
Page 9: Drawing copyright © Robbrecht en Daem Architecten/Witherford Watson Mann Architects, based on a measured survey by Michael Gallie and Partners
Pages 10 and 15: photographs by Tom Vaneynde
Page 22: photograph by Scott Livingstone
Pages 27–33: silhouette drawings by Neil Wedman
Pages 23–35: Erasmus' letters and map of "Erasmus' Odyssey reproduced from *The Praise of Folly and Other Writings* by Desiderius Erasmus, translated by Robert M. Adams. Copyright © 1989 by W. W. Norton & Company, Inc. Used by permission of W. W. Norton & Company, Inc.
Pages 45, 46 and back cover: Valentine Blacque contributions originally published in "The Equestrian Monuments of the World," New York, 1913

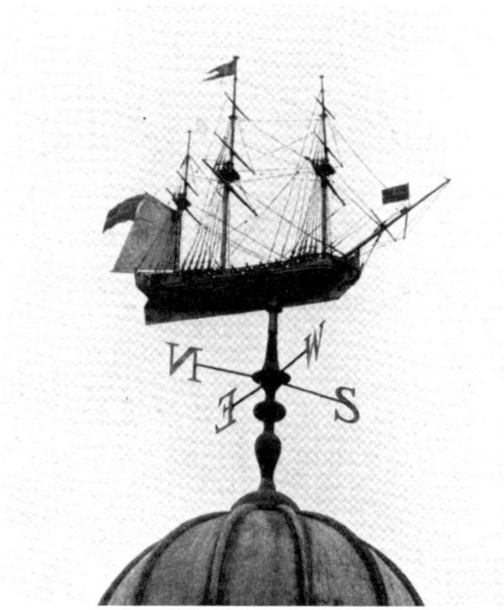

Sir Cloudesley Shovel's frigate
as the vane of Rochester Guildhall

The Whitechapel Gallery would like to thank the following people for their help in bringing the weathervane to the Whitechapel: Rodney Graham, Scott Livingstone, Shannon Oksanen and Derek Root; Donald Young, Emily Letourneau and the Donald Young Gallery, Chicago; Dick Polich at Polich Tallix Fine Art Foundry; Price and Myers, Structural Engineers; Max Fordham LLP, Service Engineers; Whitechapel Gallery Project Team; Robbrecht en Daem Architecten; Witherford Watson Mann Architects; Kier Wallis, Building Contractors. The Whitechapel would also like to thank Arts Council England and Canada House Arts Trust for their support of this project